# MONEY FREEDOM

# MONEY FREEDOM

## FINDING YOUR INNER SOURCE OF WEALTH

by Patricia Remele

A.R.E. Press • Virginia Beach • Virginia

A.R.E. Press
Sixty-Eighth & Atlantic Avenue
P.O. Box 656
Virginia Beach, VA 23451-0656

Library of Congress Cataloging-in-Publication Data
Remele, Patricia, 1938-
    Money freedom : finding your inner source of wealth / by
Patricia Remele.
        p.   cm.
    ISBN 0-87604-333-3
    1. Money—Psychological aspects. I. Title.
HG222.3.R46   1995
332.024—dc20                                      94-44279

Cover design by Richard Boyle

# Dedication

To my fellow travelers on the journey

# CONTENTS

# Acknowledgments

My deepest thanks to all of you who expressed your desire to read my book and kept encouraging me to write and finish it. Your support was crucial to me, more than you can imagine. There are far too many of you to name, but you know who you are. My deepest gratitude to you all. My thanks also to the people who read portions of the book and gave me useful feedback.

Thank you to my editor Richard Heinberg for his wisdom and editing talents. Also, my thanks to Helen Soos, who began writing the book with me for a short while and then moved to Niger, Africa.

I am infinitely grateful to *A Course in Miracles*, a psychological, spiritual book of universal truths, that has helped me and continues to help me to transform my life. I would also like to acknowledge Tom Carpenter, author of *Dialogue on Awakening*, who has a way of expressing concepts that gives me a whole new perspective and clarity. My gratitude also to my earlier teachers: Arnold Patent, Grady Clare Porter and the Forum. Also, I acknowledge Paul Ferrini, author and creator of the Miracles Community Network, for all the work he has done in facilitating growth and communication for many of us.

# INTRODUCTION

*MONEY FREEDOM* is a product of my journey from feeling powerless—which was reflected in a $20,000 negative cash flow the year after my divorce—to my taking charge of my life, which was reflected three years later in my earning $600,000 that year.

My reason for writing the book is to share the breakthroughs and tools that have enabled me to transform my life. I have seen these tools help others and my vision is that we may all enjoy happy, abundant lives. I am deeply thankful that I had the opportunity to learn how to transform my life and I am happy to have this opportunity to share with you. I believe in a world where we all help each other.

This book is about far more than money. It is about living in a new way—happy, and free from worries about money. It is a blueprint for having what we choose in life. The purpose of this book is not to state "truths"; rather, it is to point the way to letting go of old perceptions and living in an open place of infinite possibility.

I am not special. I am not different from you. When we get to our core essence, we are the same. You can do anything that I can do. How you express money freedom in your outer life would look different, but money freedom is a way of being that all of us can experience.

If you don't agree with some of the concepts, please try them anyway. You don't have to believe them for them to work for you in retraining your mind and feelings.

It has been a great joy for me to write this book. It has clarified and reinforced for me my new way of mastery. I feel much gratitude for my life as it is now. I hope that this book brings you the kind of joy that I experience from money freedom and life mastery.

My transformation has brought a change in a feeling quality of my life as well as a shift in how I see myself, money, and the world. The following poem expresses the money freedom experience.

### Money Freedom

I am free
Money has no power over me
I am free
I know I have enough
I am free
I have no lack
I am free
I don't need to strive for more
I am free
Money is my friend and servant
I am free
The master of my life
I am free
My whole, abundant self.

I am free
Nothing external has power over me
I am free
The past is gone and buried
I am free
I accept my worthiness
I am free
I trust myself, I trust the world
I am free
I feel connected to my source
I am free
Joyful, safe, and loved.

Money freedom is
Not having to think about money
Money freedom is
I am enough; I have enough
Money freedom is
Money being my friendly servant
Money freedom is
A state of infinite possibilities.

# 1

# Playing with Money Differently

*The significant problems we face cannot be solved at the same level of thinking we were at when we created them.*
—Albert Einstein

*Wealth does not reside in material possession. Wealth resides in the mind. It is a thought.*
—Robert Allen, *Creating Wealth*

THE PURPOSE of this book is to enable you to have wealth and inner power for a lifetime by transforming your basic worldview.

The real solution to the problem of lack of money does not lie at the level of the problem. We can go for the quick fix classes on how to buy a house with no money down; books about risk-free investments; memberships in multi-level marketing programs; second or third jobs; offshore bank accounts. But whatever we do, the pattern of our relationship to wealth tends to reassert itself. The solution comes from a change in our fundamental attitudes toward, and hence our relationship with, power and wealth. As the saying goes, "Give a man a fish and you feed him for a day. Teach a man to fish and you feed him for a lifetime."

The lack of money can block you from achieving what you choose to do in life. Many people who are deeply committed to service are hampered from accomplishing their worthwhile goals by lack of money. Others have visions of personal fulfillment that are never met because they don't have the money with which to realize their visions. This is not freedom. Money freedom comes from knowing that *you* are the source of your power and that money is your tool.

We often make assumptions that limit our possibilities. For example, it was long believed that the mile could not be run in less than four minutes. When Roger Bannister broke the four-minute barrier, it changed everyone's beliefs immediately. The next year, thirty-seven other people equaled or bettered his feat. In the following year three hundred runners ran the four-minute mile. What had happened? The human body hadn't changed. There was no breakthrough in technology. The only change that had taken place was in people's minds. Today we are ready for a similar breakthrough in our assumptions about power and money.

*The single underlying belief that most disempowers us is that our lives are controlled by circumstances*—money, our boss, our education, our past, our national origin, our geographical location, our social status. And the single factor we most often see as being in charge of our lives is money.

This book will teach you the secret of inner power, and it will wean you from dependence on any outside source of authority.

Money and power are closely intertwined in our society. Some people strive for money because they think it will bring them power. Other people sabotage their relationship with money because they are afraid of the negative aspects of power. Using the tools in this book, you will discover that money is a willing servant, ready to help you in living a fulfilled life. You will discover *yourself* as the source of power and authority in your life, and you will free yourself from the tyranny of external circumstances.

At the beginning of each chapter you will see a brief, one-sentence example of the LIMITED approach that keeps us dependent, and the EMPOWERED approach, which frees us from control by circumstances and puts us in charge of our lives. The principal LESSON of the chapter is also summarized here.

Even if you don't agree with some of the ideas in this book, I invite you to keep an open mind. Sometimes ideas we disagree with are still helpful to us in some way. I invite you to see this as a joyful opportunity and as an adventure in challenging and changing perspectives.

## My Journey to Financial Empowerment

*The real voyage of discovery consists not in seeing new landscapes but in having new eyes.*—Marcel Proust

This book is the result of my own self-empowerment journey. I am sharing my story with you because many people have told me that it inspired them to transform their own lives. I am not a special person in the sense that I've done something that no one else can do. In fact, I believe that the option of transformation is available to us all.

I grew up in a middle-class family. There wasn't a lot of fear about money, nor was there a sense of freedom or empowerment. Money came from a faceless bureaucracy in New York City, where my father worked as an accountant. We lived comfortably and conservatively.

My relationship with money was a little more direct in my marriage. My husband feared not having money, and he was determined to save money and make some investments. He opened his own restaurant and it was successful. We lived very frugally, using the money we brought in to invest in some real estate.

My marriage lasted twenty years. At the end of that time, I felt like a stuck and powerless victim, subject to my husband's control. In my "poor me" state I saw the world through a set of blinders that permitted little possibility of change. I began seeing a marriage counselor. I realized that an immediate step I could take to free myself and to begin to take charge of my life would be to get divorced. I got divorced in 1984.

On my own, I felt anxious and scared, especially about supporting myself financially. I had worked as a writer for several years after college, but most of my life had been spent working in my husband's business and in real estate on the side. Now, suddenly, I was responsible for my own financial affairs. I had some assets, but I wasn't receiving alimony or child support. My former husband was not working at the time. I was working part time as a writer for the U.S. Senate Finance Committee, but that didn't generate enough income to support me, nor could I see much future in the job: I didn't have the graduate degrees and experience needed in order to move to the higher-paying positions in my office; and, since I had two teenage children at home, I didn't want to work the long hours that were the norm for the full-time professionals there. That first year I was single again, I had a $20,000 negative cash flow. My life was controlled by the lack of money.

At the same time, I found that my thinking was beginning to change. One by one, books on personal growth and human potential magically presented themselves to me at just the right time. Soon I was seeking out and devouring this kind of material. I began to understand that I could be in charge of my life, and I started to look at my financial world from a broader perspective. What could I do financially to empower myself? After much encouragement from a close friend, I decided to see if I could make a living by buying properties at foreclosure auctions on the courthouse steps, doing superficial repairs—painting and installing new carpeting—and reselling them.

I had taken a course on foreclosures a few years previously. I had bought one house in foreclosure with my husband while I was married, but we didn't do well on the property. However, I decided to give it another try in my spare time while continuing with my job. I made friends with people who were doing this for a living. I asked lots of questions. I studied the market.

I was able to borrow some cash by putting a second trust line of credit on my house. My first purchase was an inexpensive condominium that I was able to sell for a profit. That gave me the confidence to take the risk and quit my job.

## Money as a Mirror

*Physical conditions—whether pertaining to social, to money, to station in life, to likes and dislikes—are the application of those mental images builded within the body, seated, guided, directed, by the spiritual . . . (349-4)*

When I began my new endeavor I still felt anxious and insecure. These attitudes translated into the outer action of being afraid to bid high enough to get any properties. There didn't seem to be any bargains in the inexpensive properties, and I didn't have enough money or credit to buy an expensive property. When you buy a house in foreclosure, you have to come up with the full amount of cash in ten to fifteen days, so there is no time to get a conventional mortgage. At this point, I had jumped in with both feet, but really wasn't getting anywhere. Bills kept piling up, but my income was nil.

At this low point in my financial affairs, I was fortunate to attend an intensive personal growth weekend workshop in which we, the participants, were given the *experience* of being in charge of our lives. Afterward I felt excited and empowered. I began to trust that I had the power to change my life by changing how I thought and felt about things. I realized that I could accept my fear consciously and then choose to do what I wanted, regardless of the fear.

The Monday after the workshop I was still feeling inspired. I got in touch with a friend who had considerable financial resources, and offered her the opportunity to share in my profits if she would become a partner with me in purchasing an expensive house. Two days later I attended a foreclosure auction and bought the scariest house of my career. The house was in a great location, but it was a total wreck. One of the other bidders told me that he and his partner had wanted the house but they knew that I was going to buy it no matter what, so they stopped bidding so as not to run me up. While I was bidding, I had a sense of myself as twenty feet tall, towering over all the other bidders. After I had bought the house, I felt both scared and exhilarated. I had gone beyond my fear of risk. I immediately went for a run in order to dispel the strong emotions flooding through my body.

I attended the follow-up meeting on the workshop and realized how dramatically the shift in my belief system had empowered me. I felt confident that I could sell the house I had bought within a few months, so I signed up for a more extensive two-weekend workshop three months away.

The house needed so much work that I didn't know where to start or what to do. I felt intimidated by the project. So I did a little painting and advertised it the next weekend as a unique opportunity to buy inexpensively a mini-estate that needed work. I sold it immediately and made a profit of $35,000. I had conquered my fear and had shifted my perception of myself, my opportunities, and money in general. I had begun to be in charge of my life instead of seeing other people and things as being in charge of me. Although I didn't realize it then, I had begun to use money as a feedback signal in my self-empowerment journey.

I continued to use money to mirror what was happening in my inner life. At one point, I had not made any money for five months. I was in the turmoil of a romantic relationship that wasn't working. I then consciously made another shift in my life. I broke up the turmoil and the relationship. I went back to studying my personal-growth and spiritual books. I began to feel good about myself and to reconnect with myself as the source of my power.

I made a decision to go to an Arnold Patent workshop

across the country in Los Angeles. I bought a workshop ticket and an airline ticket, which was a financial stretch at the time. However, I had decided to be in charge of my life again. I had taken a stand to make a breakthrough in my life, and I had taken the action of buying the tickets. This act of trust was immediately reflected in my financial situation. I got two good buys on houses in the next ten days that soon made me a profit of about $65,000. I was again using money as a feedback mechanism to reward my inner thought breakthroughs.

I bought only houses that were sold at auction. They were often vacant. However, if there were residents in them, I committed myself to making the people glad that it was I who had bought the house rather than one of the other bidders. I supported them emotionally and financially through their period of transition.

Sometimes I seemed to get a property just to help someone. I remember an occupied condominium that would not sell. My house-fixing friend and I decided to support the previous owner, who was obviously in rough shape. In conversation, he admitted that he was an alcoholic, and we talked him into joining Alcoholics Anonymous. One night a few weeks later he called me in tears of joy to thank me for enabling him finally to tell his father the truth about his life. For me, there was nothing hard-nosed about the real estate business. I made good profits and I did what I felt was right. There was no conflict.

During this period I noticed that my ability to sell houses seemed to reflect my feelings about myself. In the beginning, I had to do a lot of work on my houses to get them into good enough shape to sell. During a period when I was especially down on myself, a house that I had done a tremendous amount of work on finally sold—only to be superficially criticized by a home inspector, causing the sale to fall through. It was four more months before I found another buyer.

On the other hand, when I accepted and loved myself just
as I was, this attitude was mirrored in my houses, which
tended to be accepted just the way *they* were. When I was at
the peak of this feeling, people would buy my houses in any
condition the minute I put them on the market.

## Sharing the Miracle of Abundance

A friend, who had been a wise and beloved spiritual
teacher to me and many other people, was in financial
trouble. I really wanted to help her, so I asked my higher
power (some people would say "higher self") to assist me to
do this. I said, "If I am able to buy a house within the next
two weeks, I will see it as a sign that I am supposed to use
the money to help her and I will give her half the profits."

Strange things happened in the bidding for the next
house. One woman who would have bid it high was five
minutes late. Another was sick. One power bidder got into
an argument with his partner and accidentally missed the
last bid. I got a great deal on the house and made twice the
profit I ordinarily would have expected.

I shared this story with a friend, who asked if I would be
willing to see if I could raise funds for a Soviet-American
Citizens Summit project, which needed money. After discussing the idea with the event's sponsors, Barbara Marx
Hubbard and Rama Vernon, I decided to give it a try.

I wrote out a request to my higher power, stipulating that
I would again split the proceeds fifty-fifty. I did not put limits on the amount, nor on the way it should appear, since I
had learned by that time simply to trust higher wisdom to
act through me in its own way. Had I made such stipula-
tions, I certainly would not have asked for (nor probably
gotten) more than $25,000.

I then went white-water rafting in the Grand Canyon for
two weeks. The everyday world quickly receded from my
mind. I felt peaceful, nourished by the magnificent beauty

of the canyon. I learned to surrender my fears, and to trust on a new level. I learned that you cannot run a river according to a preset plan. The only way to run a river is to read the water and go with the flow. I was learning to tune in to the flow, to trust, and to let go. This white-water experience proved to be a good metaphor for the next step in my life.

Shortly after I returned home, I received a strong intuitive message that the stock market was going to crash on October 19, 1987. Three years earlier, I wouldn't have even heard the message. However, my intuition had worked well when it came to buying houses. But I had never given much attention to the stock market.

Since I had committed myself to the path of personal growth and spiritual work, I had been consciously listening to my intuition, my inner voice. I had learned to check whether my frequent hunches originated with higher wisdom, or with random rumblings of my unconscious mind. I examined my feelings, and was clear that I was in the peace-trust-love state versus the anxiety-fear state. I was clear that I was making the right choice in deciding to serve these people and this cause. So I decided to act on the information.

Though I didn't know much about the stock market, my former husband had told me about a stock market service that was recommending put and call options on the Standard and Poors Index. I learned that these options are rights to buy or sell at a specific price based on the stock market averages in the particular index one buys. It is investing on the market as a whole versus a specific stock. The leverage was high and the risk limited to the amount invested. I went to his broker, Richard, and asked him which options he would buy if the stock market were going to crash in a week. Richard told me—and advised me strongly not to throw my money away. I bought the options and Richard circled them in the newspaper so I could find them. That week I kept buying more and more as the feeling of impending crash strengthened. I invested a total of $10,000.

On Monday, my broker called and said that my options were worth a half a million dollars. He explained that each option was a market basket that was multiplied by 100, which I had not realized before. I had unwittingly used the instrument with the highest leverage during the largest market crash of modern times. And I did not have any influential friends in high places. To add to that, my real estate earnings that year were over $100,000. I divided 50% of my earnings between a foundation and the Citizens Summit.

The experience was certainly exhilarating, but also upsetting, as it didn't fit my expectations. The magnitude of the event threw me off balance. I began to feel anxious, and then I made some poor investments, which only reflected my inner turmoil. I hadn't prepared myself for this level of prosperity. My experience was similar to that of many lottery winners, who unconsciously choose to lose most of their new-found wealth in order to return to their more familiar, and therefore more comfortable, financial status.

However, I kept enough wealth to support an expanded vision of my life's purpose. I moved into a new network of people, many of whom were public speakers and published authors. I began to see that I had provided myself with this experience in order to shove myself out of my small puddle and into a larger pond. People's strong response to my story and their requests to learn more inspired me to begin writing this book. And, I realized, I had already given myself a publisher's advance.

As I looked back on the previous few years, I realized that I had gone from feeling anxious, insecure, and powerless to feeling free, relaxed, in charge of my life, and financially abundant. It was only as I had begun to feel differently about myself, money, and power that my financial situation changed dramatically. I had begun to feel that I was in charge of my life. And I knew that other people could achieve the same money freedom I had, if only they would undertake a similar process of internal change.

## Discovering Where You Are Now

*Know the truth, and the truth shall make you free.*
*—John 8:32*

Suppose you lived in Washington, D.C., and you packed your bags and loaded them into your car, intending to drive to San Francisco. If you pretended to be in Chicago and chose your maps accordingly, you would become lost immediately.

Fooling ourselves about the place from which we're starting makes arriving at our destination impossible. Yet this is what most of us do in various areas of our lives. We pretend that everything is fine with our jobs or our marriages while neglecting deep-seated problems. Most of us know someone who seemed to have a good marriage, but then told us after a surprise divorce how unhappy he or she had been for the previous five years.

*The first step toward achieving our goal is honestly assessing where we are in life in relation to where we choose to be.* But in order to do so, we may need to break out of habitual patterns of perception or nonperception that can blind us to reality.

Psychologists Joseph and David Weisel performed an experiment with newborn kittens. As the kittens began to open their eyes, the psychologists separated them into three groups and placed each in a carefully controlled environment. The first group was put in a white box with horizontal stripes, the second group in a white box with vertical stripes, and the third in a box that was all white. They were kept there for the critical few days during which sight develops.

Later, when they were let loose, the kittens' sight was limited to what they had seen the first few days. The first group couldn't see vertical stripes and bumped into chair and table legs. The second group could see only vertical stripes.

The third group was the most disoriented, because all they could see was empty space, with no defining features.

Although some of our early human programming in seeing the world may not be as obvious as this, the concepts we were taught about wealth and power are frequently just as bizarre. They limit our perceptions as adults, sabotaging our present-day actions. And they're hard to spot, since from childhood we've been trained to treat them as part of the furniture. They are a given part of our worldview, and they are not open to question until we shift our perspective. That's what this book is all about. Unlike the kittens, we can change our perceptions of the world; we can pry out the perceptions that limit our relationship to money and power, and transform them.

Take a minute and ask yourself, "What would be the consequences if I had wealth?" Write down the answers that come to mind. Now ask, "What would happen if I had power?" You may find that these questions bring up fears and doubts, along with the more positive feelings and images that you might expect. These fears and doubts are blocking you from experiencing abundance and power. They come from confusing abundance with the stockpiling of wealth; from confusing inner power with power over others.

The following self-assessment will help you define the areas in which your belief systems may be sabotaging you. Then we can identify and transform limiting beliefs in:

> The way you see money;
> The way you see power;
> The way you see the world;
> The way you see yourself.

*Exercise*

## Money and Power Self-Assessment

Here's a chance to get a quick profile of how you ooo your self in relation to money freedom.

Read each statement below, and rate your response on a scale from 0 to 5, low to high agreement. If you don't relate to the attitude exemplified in the statement, circle the 0. If you feel that it describes you perfectly, circle the 5. Write down your first impressions, quickly; don't take time to ponder the statement deeply.

While you are doing the assessment, take careful note of your responses. If you feel a high degree of emotional charge while reading a statement, put a star next to it so that you can return to it later. Also, be aware of the feeling that the statements bring forth. Being aware of our feelings is an essential tool in transforming ourselves to a state of money freedom.

This is not meant to be an exhaustive, scientific analysis; it is a tool for you to use in reflecting on your present attitudes. Notice whether you are tempted to give the "correct" answer, even if it's stretching the truth.

I used to give this self-assessment in the form of a quiz and it was useful in showing up patterns of denial. For example, a participant in one of my workshops got the highest score of anyone that day. It might have appeared that she had no money issues to deal with. However, I happened to know that she had recently been forced to declare bankruptcy, and she could not even afford a car. Her general pattern in life was to deny reality, and her test scores faithfully reflected that pattern. Another participant told me that he had wanted to cheat in order to make his scores look better. But he realized that the purpose of the quiz was to help him discover his own attitudes about money, and that cheating would make the scores useless to him.

You may wish to photocopy this survey and work on a copy, so that you can take it again after you have finished reading this book and doing the exercises outlined later on.

## Money Freedom Self-Assessment

### *Section A—Money*

#### Limiting Beliefs—Money

0  1  2  3  4  5   I don't understand how money works.

0  1  2  3  4  5   I'd rather be poor, and be able to hold my head up high, than to sell out to money.

0  1  2  3  4  5   You have to sacrifice (<u>fill in the blank</u>) to get money.

0  1  2  3  4  5   Making money is a struggle.

0  1  2  3  4  5   Money separates you from your family and friends.

0  1  2  3  4  5   We are not supposed to enjoy money.

#### Empowering Beliefs—Money

0  1  2  3  4  5   Money is my friend.

0  1  2  3  4  5   I like to use money to help others.

0  1  2  3  4  5   Money supports me to do what I want to do.

0  1  2  3  4  5   Money is a tool.

0  1  2  3  4  5   Money means freedom.

0  1  2  3  4  5   Money is neutral. I give it the meaning it has for me.

0  1  2  3  4  5   Money flows naturally through my life.

### *Section B—World*

#### Limiting Beliefs—World

0  1  2  3  4  5   I am tired of being cheated.

0  1  2  3  4  5   I worry about not having enough money.

0  1  2  3  4  5   Life isn't fair.

0  1  2  3  4  5  We have to fight for our share.
0  1  2  3  4  5  There is only so much, and the rich hog it.
0  1  2  3  4  5  Nobody is going to take care of me except me.
0  1  2  3  4  5  Never let your guard down.

### Empowering Beliefs—World

0  1  2  3  4  5  Give unto others as you would have them give unto you.
0  1  2  3  4  5  We reap what we sow.
0  1  2  3  4  5  I feel accepted and supported.
0  1  2  3  4  5  I enjoy sharing my money with others.
0  1  2  3  4  5  I feel confident about the future.
0  1  2  3  4  5  Whenever I need help, someone seems to come along and give me what I need.
0  1  2  3  4  5  I believe that the Universe is benevolent.
0  1  2  3  4  5  The world is a safe place.
0  1  2  3  4  5  I trust others and the world in general.
0  1  2  3  4  5  There is enough if we use our resources differently.
0  1  2  3  4  5  The world is a mutual-support system.
0  1  2  3  4  5  I enjoy supporting others.

## *Section C—Self*

### Limiting Beliefs—Self

0  1  2  3  4  5  I'm not worthy.
0  1  2  3  4  5  I always seem to mess things up.
0  1  2  3  4  5  I had a lousy upbringing.
0  1  2  3  4  5  I always get the short end of the stick.
0  1  2  3  4  5  What is the use of struggling when you always get beat down?
0  1  2  3  4  5  I feel like I can't have money.
0  1  2  3  4  5  There are limited opportunities for a person like me.

### Empowering Beliefs—Self

0  1  2  3  4  5  I feel in control of my life.
0  1  2  3  4  5  I feel grateful that I have enough.
0  1  2  3  4  5  I deserve to be wealthy.
0  1  2  3  4  5  I can do whatever I make up my mind to do.
0  1  2  3  4  5  I have a deep sense that I will always be all right financially.
0  1  2  3  4  5  Money always comes easily to me.
0  1  2  3  4  5  I trust my own judgment.
0  1  2  3  4  5  I listen to my intuition.
0  1  2  3  4  5  I am successful.
0  1  2  3  4  5  I am comfortable playing big in the world.
0  1  2  3  4  5  I enjoy taking risks.
0  1  2  3  4  5  I can be abundant and fulfilled.
0  1  2  3  4  5  I can do what I love and receive abundant financial support.

Look back over your numbers and notice where you have limiting beliefs. Pay special attention to the chapters focusing on these areas.

## Setting Our Inner Genie Free

*Most people live, whether physically, intellectually or morally, in a very restricted circle of their potential being. They make use of a very small portion of their possible consciousness, of their soul's resources in general, much like a man who, out of his whole bodily organism, should get into a habit of using and moving only his little finger. Great emergencies and crises show us how much greater our vital resources are than we had supposed.—William James*

*[The peak performers] did what others can learn to do. They saw beyond the probable by envisioning the pos-*

*sible: a state of affairs that they desired to bring about, and believed in. Then they found their place, took a stand.*—Charles Garfield, *Peak Performers: The New Heroes of American Business*

Remember the old tale of Aladdin and his lamp? An impoverished, fatherless lad called Aladdin found an old copper lamp. By accident, he discovered that when the lamp was rubbed, a genie would appear, saying: "What wouldst thou have? I am ready to obey thee as thy slave, and the slave of all who have the lamp in their hands."

Aladdin prospered with his wonderful lamp. He saw in the lamp a path to wealth and happiness. He summoned riches, a palace, and the sultan's daughter as a bride. He lived a contented, abundant life. His mother, however, was unable to share his prosperity and continued to live in poverty.

The genie-in-the-lamp motif has been distorted by our culture and trivialized by television; yet the Persian tales from which the fable of Aladdin's lamp was drawn are teaching stories based on ancient Sufi wisdom. This story shows how to manifest what we want in life. Aladdin was a poor boy, but he desired riches, power, and love. He empowered himself to have the things that he wanted by drawing to himself a magical tool. He lived happily. He did not misuse the power of the lamp by seeking to dominate others.

Notice that the genie said that he was the slave of all those who had the lamp in their hands. Aladdin's mother could also have used the lamp to bring herself riches and power, but her thought system was mired in poverty and drudgery. We can use our lamp, or we can stay stuck in our old perceptions of the world. The choice is ours.

You have just acquired an Aladdin's lamp. It comes free with this book. You have in your hands the instruction manual for using your Aladdin's lamp to produce the riches you want.

Your Aladdin's lamp is a magical tool called empowerment. It enables you to produce riches and inner power. You can be rich in any area of your life—in work, love, friendships, beauty, or creativity.

The genie who is bound to serve your desires is your mind. The word *genie* comes from the same root as the word *genius*. Our mind is our inner genius, and the magic of empowerment sets it free from unconscious conditioning that tends to mire us down in self-destructive habits and attitudes.

As an empowered person, you consciously control your mind to produce the results you choose. When you learn to recognize sabotaging beliefs and feelings that are blocking your path to riches, you then have the opportunity to transform these old beliefs into empowerment attitudes.

Higher wisdom taps sources of knowledge beyond our everyday consciousness. William James estimated that we habitually use no more than 5% of our intelligence, leaving a vast potential untapped. Carl Jung spoke of this untapped reservoir as the collective unconscious. Others have referred to it as higher power, Universal Mind, God, infinite intelligence, Atman, the Force, or the superconscious. It doesn't matter how we conceptualize it. There is unlimited power available to us when we reach beyond everyday consciousness.

Quantum physics tells us that, beneath the surface world of appearances as organized and perceived by our human senses, reality is composed of interconnected, dynamic energy patterns. Our superconscious mind is part of this energy matrix. This is the realm of the genie. We can learn to access it to serve our purposes.

The first step in summoning your genie is to remember that your genius is *within* you. The next steps are those that Aladdin took: he knew what he desired; he asked for it; and he believed that what he asked for would be given to him. This is how we access the power of our superconscious and subconscious minds.

Jesus taught the same method for producing what you desire. He said, "What things soever ye desire, when ye pray, believe that ye receive them, and ye shall have them." (Mark 11:24) Notice the same course of action: desire, ask, and believe.

One caveat: Sometimes, on a higher level, it isn't appropriate for us to get everything we want. Remember King Midas, who desired to turn everything he touched to gold? When he went to pick his roses they turned to gold. Then he hugged his beloved daughter and she turned to gold. When I ask for anything, I always request that it work according to the highest good.

Here are the steps involved in communicating with your genie mind:

1. *Desire* the riches;
2. *Ask* for or choose to have riches, according to your highest good;
3. *Believe* that you can have the riches;
4. *Transform* old sabotaging thoughts and feelings;
5. *Feel* as though you already have your desire;
6. *Act* on the new expectancy.

Each step carries the stipulation that it be for the highest good.

When you realize that power lies within you, you can fulfill your desires for the rest of your life, and share this abundant teaching with others. Genie power is available to everyone.

*Exercise*

## Costs and Benefits

Sit quietly and relax your body. You may wish to meditate or to listen to peaceful music. Now take a piece of paper and answer the following questions.

1. What would it feel like to have sufficient money

to support you in doing what you choose?

2. What is blocking you? What fears and resistances came up when you contemplated the first question?

3. What does it cost you to have less than enough money in your life?

4. What are the payoffs you get for maintaining your present condition?

5. What would be the benefits to having sufficient money?

6. Are you willing to change your belief system and your relationship to money?

7. What could you, as an individual, do to change your relationship to money?

   If you feel ready to change your position, go ahead and answer the question. If you aren't quite ready, *pretend* that you felt that the costs of your old position outweighed the benefits and that you are now deciding to transform your perception so as to allow there to be a sufficiency of money in your life.

8. What would your life look like five years from now if you had sufficient money to be free to live from choice?

*Exercise*

## Imagining an Unlimited Source

Let's play *what if.* Allow yourself to imagine that you have an unlimited source of money to serve you. Pretend that you have just won the lottery. You immediately receive a million dollars and will receive $500,000 a year for the next twenty years.

Ask yourself, "If I had this unlimited source of money, how

would I choose to live my life?" Write down your answers.

After you have satisfied your material needs and those of the people close to you, expand to the larger context. Imagine that you no longer have to spend time and energy making money. Ask yourself, "How would I choose to live my life? What is my purpose? How would the access to unlimited wealth expand my purpose? How could I use money to serve others? How could I use money to serve the planet?"

Describe what your life is like five years from now with an unlimited source of wealth. What are you doing? How are you spending your time? What have you done over the past five years? How do you feel? How do you feel about money? How do you feel about yourself? How do you see the world in relation to you?

*Exercise*

# Training Our Mind to Allow New Possibilities (The NLP *Believe* Technique)

There is a science of directing and training the brain called Neuro-Linguistic Programming (NLP), pioneered by John Grinder and Richard Bandler. NLP shows us how we can train our nervous system to do what we choose. It is the study of using verbal and nonverbal language effectively to program our mind.

One of Grinder and Bandler's discoveries is that there is an area of the mind in which we store thoughts that we believe.

Say to yourself, "My name is (your name) and I live at (your address)." As you are saying this, ask yourself, Where are those thoughts stored in my mind? If you have trouble locating the spot, have someone watch your eyes as you repeat your name and address. Your eyes will look toward that part of the brain. That is where you store whatever you *believe*. You may find that it is a specific spot in the upper right part of your brain.

Now say to yourself, "I am going to turn purple tomorrow." Where does that thought register? That is the *doubt* section of your mind.

NLP studies show the relationship between our physiology—how we hold our body, how we breathe, how we hold our head and shoulders, our facial expressions, and how we move—and our emotional and mental state. As an example, try the following: Hang your head down. Tense your neck and hunch your shoulders. Frown. Now say, "I feel a sense of wealth and inner power." What happens? Do you feel your body position negating the statement?

As we place new thoughts in the *believe* part of our minds, it is important to have the body in a *believe* position also. Take a deep breath. Sit up straight. Look up. Let your shoulders relax. Smile. See your body looking strong and expanded. Tune in to the way your body feels. Feel a sense of inner power. *This is the physical posture we will use as we do the mind training exercises at the end of each chapter.*

Now tell yourself: *"I can see money differently."* Take a deep breath. Place your body in the *believe* position and place that statement in the *believe* portion of your mind.

Repeat the statement five times now. Continue repeating it as often as feels appropriate in order for you to really get it.

Take any "yes, but" thoughts that pop up and place them in the *doubt* section of your mind. Do this with a neutral body position.

Focus your continuing attention on reaffirming your choice in the believe section of your mind. It is important to put the emphasis on what you choose. Do this exercise whenever a limiting thought comes up. Taking charge of your belief system is a skill that improves with repetition and practice.

*They can because they think they can.*—Virgil

# 2

# TAKING CHARGE OF MONEY

*Until one is committed there is hesitancy, the chance to draw back, always ineffectiveness. Concerning all acts of initiative (and creation), there is one elementary truth the ignorance of which kills countless ideas and splendid plans: that the moment one definitely commits oneself then Providence moves too. All sorts of things occur to help one that would never otherwise have occurred. A whole stream of events issues from the decision, raising in one's favor all manner of unforeseen incidents and meetings and material assistance which no man could have dreamt would have come his way.*
  —W. H. Murray, *The Scottish Himalayan Expedition*

*LIMITED:* I can never do what is really important to me because I lack the money.

*EMPOWERED:* I will decide what I need to do to be happy and fulfilled, and I WILL have the money and resources I need to do it.

*LESSON:* I declare that I am in charge of money.

MOST PEOPLE in our society are convinced that money has a great deal of power over our lives. We see money as having the power to make us happy or to make us unhappy. In a recent survey reported by *Parade* magazine, 80% of the people polled reported that their lives were at least "somewhat controlled" by money.

Are you in charge of your life? Do you do what you want to do, or does money control your decisions? If life were a huge chessboard, would you be moving money around as your pawn, or would money be moving you around? Are you doing what you love to do for a living, or is money dictating what you do? Are you striving to accomplish something greater than making money? Are you being hampered by a lack of money? Are you playing as powerfully in the world as you want, or is a shortfall of money keeping you or your organization from doing everything you envision? Do you want to go back to school, change jobs, travel, or move to a new place, and believe that you can't because money won't let you? If you answered "Yes" to many of these questions, then for you it is true that, as Ralph Waldo Emerson once observed, "Things are in the saddle and ride mankind."

## Who Is in Charge—Money or Me?

*(In a shipwreck) one of the passengers fastened a belt around him with two hundred pounds of gold on it, with which he was afterwards found at the bottom. Now, as he was sinking—had he the gold? Or had the gold him?*—John Ruskin

From the time we are infants, we are trained to view external forces as controlling our lives. By the time we are adults money has usually become the most common focus for our perceptions of limitation, but any other external factor will do. How many times have you said (you fill in the blanks):

I can't _____ because _____.
I can't _____ because _____.
I can't _____ because _____.

The phrase following every "because" indicates something that you have given power over your life. It may be money, your job, your boss, your mate, or your position in society. Whatever it is, it blocks you from feeling powerful and doing as you choose.

We live in a society that endows money with great power. While we aren't ruled by a dictator or a foreign oppressor, we have nevertheless yielded much of our sovereignty to the subtle rulership of money. It dictates what programs we see on TV, what our newspapers and magazines print, what careers people choose, where we live. For most of us, making money consumes the majority of our time and energy.

*Brain/Mind Bulletin* reports that in the twenty-third annual survey of incoming college freshman in American colleges and universities, 72% reported that making more money was a primary reason for going to college. Our children spend twelve to twenty years of their lives in school so they can "make a good living." Money is in charge.

We decide how clean our air will be, based on the cost. We don't start with a vision of clean air and then determine how to achieve it; rather, we calculate what we can afford. Again, money is in charge.

Most of us have a limiting story about money. The variety of the stories is endless, but most can be traced to our parents' attitudes.

One man told me that his parents frequently criticized his aunt, who had money but didn't share it with the rest of the family. He realized that ever since, he had harbored an unconscious fear that if he possessed money, he would be an outcast.

A woman friend shared the story of how her mother cleaned houses for people and resented it. Her mother felt demeaned by her job and angry that their family "wasn't good enough" to have money. She accused "them" (the wealthy people) of hoarding and controlling money. Today the daughter works as a psychotherapist, yet she still does not allow herself to have much money, because she doesn't want to become one of "them."

A multimillionaire entrepreneur traced his quest to make more and more money back to his internalization of his parents' expectations that he prove himself.

While the stories are different, the theme is the same. Money is running the game and we are its pawns. *The purpose of this book is to help us reclaim the power we have given to money.*

The fish swimming in water likely does not know that there is any context in the world other than that of water. Chances are, unless we have lived part of our lives in a very different culture, our society's values are as invisible to us as water is to a fish. Only by jumping out of the water can the fish experience a new context. Only by jumping out of our society's thought system can we experience freedom from it. The pages of this book present an opportunity for us to jump out of the water, as far as money is concerned; to understand what it really is and to see the myths about money that give it such power over us.

In order to gain our freedom, we need the equivalent of a revolution. The oppressor and tyrant who must be overthrown is our own thought system, insofar as it creates and maintains the conviction that money controls us. Each of us can overthrow the tyranny of money by changing our beliefs. As we do this individually, we also help overthrow money as the controlling force in our society. We can reclaim our power to live as we choose. We can give our children the power to choose their own lives, freeing them from servitude to money.

I invite you to sign the document below. It is a Declaration of Independence from the Tyranny of Money. It is a tool for consciously acknowledging that we have given money the power to control us, and that only we can declare ourselves free.

## The Declaration of Independence from the Tyranny of Money

We hold these truths to be self-evident: That all persons are created equal, with a birthright of inner power and wealth, and endowed with certain inalienable rights, among which are the right to freedom from the tyranny of money, and the right to design a life that includes wealth, inner power, peace, and happiness.

That to secure these rights, money was instituted among people as a tool, deriving its power from the consent of the people, to serve their economic purposes. It is a neutral force to be used by the people to serve the people.

That should money become destructive of these ends, it is the right of the people to alter the way they perceive and use money and to institute a new vision of, and relationship with money, reclaiming their power from money and reorganizing their perception in such form, as to them shall seem most likely to effect their well-being and happiness.

## Your Personal Declaration of Independence

I, _____ , do hereby declare my personal independence from money. I recognize that I am the sole source of my wealth and power. Any power that money has is derived from me, and I hereby declare that the only power money has in my life henceforth is the power to serve me as my neutral tool.

Signed _____

Date _____

Remember the story of the child watching the parade who exclaimed, "The emperor has no clothes"? The child broke the consensual agreement on reality. We can do that, too, with regard to our society's attitude toward money.

I am not suggesting that money is bad. Money is a tool, and we decide how to use it. If we think of ourselves as water pitchers, then we can give only what we have. When a pitcher is empty, it has no water to give to thirsty people. If the water pitcher is half full, it can give only to some of the people. If the water pitcher is full and refilled from an unending supply, it can give water to all who ask. When we have no money, we cannot contribute to ourselves, to others, or to the causes in which we believe. When we are an abundant source of money, we have the freedom to follow our personal vision and to support our vision for the world. It is enjoyable to have abundance to support us in doing what we love.

Our first step toward enjoying our birthright of abundance is to understand this entity called money and the power we have given to it.

## Money, Money, Money— What Is It?

*If a man empties his purse into his head, no one can take it away from him.*—Benjamin Franklin

*Third Wave money increasingly consists of electronic pulses. It is evanescent . . . instantaneously transferred . . . monitored on the video screen. It is, in fact, virtually a video phenomenon itself. Blinking, flashing, whizzing across the planet, Third Wave money is information . . .* —Alvin Toffler, *Power Shift*

What is money? We say that:

Money talks;
Money makes the man;
Money makes the world go round;
Money corrupts.

But why is money so important to us?—when all authorities on the subject agree that *in itself, money has no meaning.* Money is simply strips of paper, chunks of metal, a line item on a bank statement, or a blip on a computer screen.

Money is a medium of exchange. It is a tool we use to obtain what we need. It is a symbol.

In the early days, people bartered one thing of value for another. Trade, growth, and the exchange of information were limited, based on interdependent relationships that people formed with each other for the purpose of exchanging goods. When barter became too unwieldy, people began to use a currency of exchange that had intrinsic value. The first forms of money were natural objects—shells threaded onto strings; armbands of feathers; pieces of handwoven cloth; artifacts made out of bronze, copper, and other metals; and even giant stone wheels. These served well as long as societies were isolated and fairly simple.

But as societies became more complex and interconnected, they needed a medium that was durable and transportable and that could be broken into different denominations of value that were universally acceptable. Thus standardized coins backed by the government came into being in Greece in the eighth century B.C., and in Rome in the fifth century B.C.

These coins were easily exchangeable but heavy, and they could be stolen. As transportation systems developed in the Middle Ages, people began to leave their coins with goldsmiths, who offered receipts that could be used much like our paper money of today. This practice expanded to the issuing of letters instructing goldsmiths to pay coins to the letter's bearer on demand; these were the forerunners of today's checks.

When the American colonists were forbidden by the British to mint gold and silver coins, they began to print paper money backed by gold or silver held in a vault by the government. Eventually (in 1963) that practice, too, gave way; now our currency is backed not by precious metals, but by the full faith of the government. Each paper dollar is an I.O.U. from Uncle Sam, but what precisely he owes us is left unspecified, since the word *dollar* has no official definition.

Moreover, banks are now required by the Federal Reserve (a private corporation administering the country's monetary system) to hold only a fraction of their deposits—as government I.O.U.s—in their vaults.

Money today is therefore purely a symbol of confidence. Our transition from currency based on substances with inherent value to paper currency with no metal backing constituted a remarkable leap of faith—though on whose part is questionable, since no vote was taken. But now, even the paper tokens are being replaced. Credit cards symbolize our potential future ability to pay for goods and services we want today. Vast sums are routinely transferred and stored as electronic blips in computer data files. Even the monthly social security checks that millions of elderly Americans formerly received by mail have been replaced by electronic data transfer. As futurist Alvin Toffler predicted years ago, we are entering an age in which the world economy is based on numbers transmitted by wire, microwave, or satellite. Money has become about as abstract as a thing can possibly be.

Money facilitates the movement of goods from place to place and motivates human workers. Money is stored energy—like oil, but lacking oil's physical reality. It is the energy of money that runs the world economic machine. To change metaphors: Money serves as the blood in the circulatory system of the world market. Just as the human body is dependent on its circulatory system for its survival, our civilization is dependent upon the market and upon money for its survival. We could not have anything like the level of material prosperity we currently enjoy without money, for the old system of barter would have prevented us from expanding commerce across great distances.

An example of what happens when shared faith in the value of money breaks down can be found in the countries of the former Soviet Union. After the breakup of the union, the government pegged the ruble at an artificially high rate of exchange. This reflected the government's wishful thinking rather than its citizens' actual degree of belief in the currency. The ruble began to trade on the black market at prices that differed radically from the official rate, dropping at times to less than 1/100th of the official exchange rate. The lesson is clear: the value of money reflects the degree of trust that people place in its worth.

As society has evolved, money has acquired a significance beyond its role as a functional tool to facilitate economic exchange. By creating a scarcity of money, society makes money function more like a commodity than a medium of exchange.

When money is seen as a commodity, and when there is fear of not having enough, some people begin to stockpile money: hoarding appears. Others accumulate enough to show off. In such cases, the natural flow of money as a medium of exchange is impeded.

In our society, people project non-economic personal values onto money, such as status, power, happiness, self-worth, and identity. This results in all sorts of confusion. Many people mistakenly think of money itself as the source of these values. The truth is that they come only from within ourselves. Currency can't substitute for them, purchase them, change them, or deny them.

Our thoughts about money affect the way we relate to it. For instance, if we think that money corrupts, whether we hold that belief consciously or unconsciously, we block money from flowing into our lives and corrupting us.

John, a client of mine, is a good artist, and he is committed to his work. He has told me about other artists he knows who have "sold out" and who paint what people will buy. He expresses admiration for great artists who suffered in poverty and were true to their art. Although professors and critics have assured him of the high quality of his paintings, virtually none have sold. He has to live with his parents even though he is in his mid-thirties. He is unhappy and restricted by his lack of money. His belief that money will corrupt his art is keeping him stuck.

Our perceptions and thoughts give money its meaning, and since we give money its meaning, we can change that meaning. When we understand this, we can change our relationship to money and design our lives as we choose. *We are the source of power in our lives—not money.*

Organizations and governments are as prone to money-blocking thoughts as individuals are. A friend of mine, who founded and runs a nonprofit organization, frequently criticizes people who have money and don't spend it in what he regards as a responsible manner. The underlying message is that his poverty proves his superiority to such people. His anger and resentment toward people with money effectively repel contributors from his organization.

During a dinner conversation, another friend was listing her goals for her organization. A prominent social activist who was at the table asked why she included prosperity as a goal. He saw prosperity as bad, because to him it implied being controlled by money. This man is a brilliant, capable person, but deeply in debt. Because he sees money as bad, he blocks it from coming into his life.

We can choose to see *ourselves* in charge of our lives. We then become the masters; money is the genie who is bound to serve us as we request. The power lies with us.

## Money Games

*Far out in the uncharted backwaters of the unfashionable end of the Western Spiral arm of the Galaxy lies a small unregarded yellow sun. Orbiting this at a distance of roughly ninety-eight million miles is an utterly insignificant little blue-green planet whose ape-descended life forms are so amazingly primitive that they still think digital watches are a pretty neat idea . . . Most of the people living on it were unhappy for pretty much of*

*the time. Many solutions were suggested for this prob-*
*lem, but most of these were largely concerned with the*
*movements of small green pieces of paper, which is odd*
*because on the whole it wasn't the small green pieces of*
*paper that were unhappy.*—Douglas Adams, *The*
*Hitchhiker's Guide to the Galaxy*

Most of us take money very seriously. Making money and
holding onto what we make consumes an enormous
amount of our energy and time. Few people treat money
with light-hearted humor. Recently, when I made a flippant
remark about money, an annoyed woman shot back: "It's
easy for you to joke because you don't have to toe the line to
bring in the money." One of the messages of this book is
that we can be relaxed about money.

The fact is that we play all kinds of games when it comes
to money. The most popular game is *Getting Our Share.*
There is a reason that the board game Monopoly has stayed
popular all these years. It represents the way most of us play
life. We work to accumulate more money so that we can
win—or at least be secure. The person with the most money,
or the most expensive possessions, wins. Getting our share
can mean having anything from a bigger house to a million-dollar mansion, from a clerk's job to the presidency of
the firm, from a position as an assistant in the lab to a full
professorship. For each person the payoff is different; the
game itself is nearly always the same. We compete to get a
larger slice of the pie than others. We compare our status
with that of others. And we admire and envy the winners in
the real-life Monopoly game—people like J. Paul Getty, Sam
Walton, and Bill Gates.

A slightly different version of the money game is called
*Impressing People with Our Possessions.* Here the emphasis
shifts from getting money to spending it and impressing
people with how much we have. A million-dollar house
makes a statement to our friends. But how many couples

with grown children really need a house the size of a small office building? The right car, say a Mercedes or a Jaguar, certainly says something about who we are—or, more accurately, how much we can afford to spend to get ourselves to and from the grocery store.

Another version of the game is *Protecting Our Share*. In this case, the point of the game is to protect our money from burglars, taxes, inflation, deflation, recession, and other economic changes. There are sophisticated burglar alarms for our houses and cars. Some rich people wear only inexpensive copies of their own jewelry, which is protected in a safe. In recent years the tax shelter business has diminished; however, tax lawyers and accountants are still doing well. A popular version of this game is the study and discussion of how to protect your wealth from economic upheavals. Editors of financial newsletters boost the circulation of their publications by promising the answer. The message: Once you've got money, you have to work hard to keep it.

A very different game is *Refusing to Sell Out*. Here, the goal is to be *better* than people who have "sold out" to commercialism. This game is based on the assumption that we have to choose whether to betray our ideals and make money, or to remain pure and poor. If someone has money, this is conclusive evidence that they have chosen the path of corruption. People who play this game live lives controlled by the lack of money.

*Playing Victim* is a meta-game. It can be played to accompany a vast range of life scripts, and affects our relationship with more than just money. In this game, I see myself as the victim of my upbringing, my spouse, my boss, my lack of education, my national origin, my geographic location, or any other factor. I may explain my circumstances by saying, "I came from a dysfunctional family"; "He took unfair advantage of me"; "You won't believe what that company did to me"; "I got a raw deal." The chronically unemployed often have long stories about how poorly they have been treated. Most of us play this game in one or another area of our lives.

*Being Instead of Having* is the non-game! In it, money is only a secondary player. A person focused on being is living as he or she chooses, without being dominated by money concerns. Such people enjoy what they are doing, whether it is composing music, assembling a machine, or writing a business plan. They are not being driven by a desired result or reward. They are at peace with themselves rather than striving for more. They are free to have or not to have money or possessions or status, because they are unattached to *having*. They use money as a tool to support themselves. They have not given up material things—only their attachment to them.

This state of *being without attachment* is taught in almost every religion. Buddhism describes it as the essence of enlightenment. Lao-tzu advises us to be like the river, which flows effortlessly without struggling or grasping. Christianity teaches us to live by faith; or, as the popular saying puts it, to "Let go and let God."

In *Peak Performers: The New Heroes of American Business,* Charles Garfield makes it clear that the primary motivation for peak performers is not money. He studied such diverse peak performers as Fran Tarkenton, football player turned entrepreneur; Steve Jobs and Stephen Wozniak, founders of Apple Computer; Thomas Watson, Sr., founder of IBM; and Tom Landry, former coach of the Dallas Cowboys football team. For these people, money was a by-product of their work. Obviously they did not *resist* making money, as each was highly successful financially. Garfield found that the common quality that these peak performers shared was a commitment to achieving something unique that they believed in and that was also important to others—whether an organization, a team, or a family.

## What Will I Allow Myself To Have?

Put your intellect aside. I want to talk to your feelings, to your subconscious mind. What feelings are you experiencing in your body? Describe them. Now read the questions below and write the first answers that pop into your head, even if they make no sense. If you answer with a simple "Yes" or "No," then ask yourself "Why?" or "Why not?" If you find yourself using your logical left brain, then write with your nondominant hand.

Do you really want to have wealth?
Are you willing to have wealth?
Is it safe for you to have wealth?
Would you know how to handle wealth well?
What do you think of people who have money?

Wealth and power often go together. In this book, when I refer to power, I mean inner power, not power over others. But because the two kinds of power are so often confused, we may find ourselves sabotaging our own effectiveness and self-worth out of a misplaced fear of imposing on others. Think of your experience of inner power as you answer these questions:

Do you really want to have power?
Are you willing to have power?
Is it safe for you to have power?
Would you know how to handle power well?
What do you think of people who have power?

One of the most effective ways to limit our sense of personal power is to not have enough money. Poverty keeps us safe. It fits the small context in which our conditioned subconscious mind thinks we "belong." It keeps us in familiar territory. It maintains our comfort zone. It is a socially ac-

ceptable excuse, like sickness. It protects us from the fear of
success or the fear of failure, which could come up if we
were to step out too far.

## The Power of Commitment

*Whatever you can do, or dream you can, begin it. Bold-
ness has genius, power, and magic in it.*—Goethe

Transformation requires making a commitment to
change. The first step toward transforming your life is to
expand your view of what is possible. That was the message
of chapter 1. The second step is to take a stand. It has been
my experience that the quote from W. H. Murray at the beginning of this chapter is very true—that "the moment one
definitely commits oneself then Providence moves too. All
sorts of things occur to help one. . . ." When I am asked to
raise money for a cause, I make a definite commitment to
my willingness and to a clear purpose. I write my commitment on paper and speak it aloud. I am clear on my intent
and I focus on my commitment for several days. And in all
my requests, commitments, and affirmations, I always add
the clause, *provided that this be for the highest good.*

As we make our commitments regarding wealth and
power, it is important to know what we are committing ourselves to. *The Oxford English Dictionary* defines *wealth* as
"the condition of being happy and prosperous; well-being;
spiritual well-being; a blessing." Yet for many people, the
word *wealth* conjures up only images of greed and corruption. The same dictionary includes in its definition of *prosperity:* "good fortune, success, well-being; the condition of
thriving." And for *abundance:* "overflowing state or condition; overflow; enough and more than enough; plentiful-
ness."

Meanings for *power* are "to be able; the ability to do or
effect something or anything; the ability to act or affect

something strongly; physical or mental strength; might; vigor, energy; force of character." Contrast these meanings with the images of overbearing imposition that come to most people's minds when they think of *power*. Again, in this book we are speaking of power as *inner power*.

When we come to the point of making a commitment, then our counter-commitments tend to come to the surface. The fact that they were unconscious heretofore gave them power over us.

Are you willing to have abundance in your life? Are you willing to make a commitment to having abundance?

*Exercise*

## Committing to Abundance

Take the largest sheet of paper you can find and, with a marking pen, write I COMMIT TO HAVING ABUNDANCE.

What feelings come up? Speak aloud the sentence you have written; do it several times. Write it several times. Pay attention to your emotions. How does your body feel? Is there tension in your shoulders?

Now write the sentence again, using the word *wealth* instead of *abundance:* I COMMIT TO HAVING WEALTH. What feelings come up?

Sit quietly and write down all the counter-thoughts that present themselves. Use no judgment, no critical analysis; just write the thoughts as soon as they pop into your mind. It may be helpful to fill in the following blanks:

I'd like to have wealth, but _____

I'd like to have wealth, but _____

I'd like to have wealth, but _____

I'd like to have wealth, but _____

(etc.)

If you have any difficulty with this exercise, then write with your nondominant hand. Now do the same exercise using the word *power* instead of *wealth:* write in large print, I COMMIT TO HAVING POWER. Then list your reservations, counter-commitments, and resistances:

I'd like to have power, but _____
I'd like to have power, but _____
I'd like to have power, but _____
I'd like to have power, but _____
(etc.)

Change begins with honestly acknowledging and accepting our resistance to change. We were all given limiting messages during childhood, and our parents were given limiting beliefs by their parents. The point is not to blame them or to blame oneself, but to accept the reality of these beliefs and childhood fears. Only by accepting them without judgment can we begin to transform them. Self-actualizing change is possible only when we accept our present situation fully. If we are blaming ourselves or others, change is difficult; but transformation springs easily from a foundation of acceptance.

I learned this the hard way. I was taught to feel that I should always be strong and look good. I had to be an outstanding student. Only by loving and accepting that part of me that is anxious and feels wounded have I been able to truly empower myself.

Think of your old, limiting ideas as children's clothes that you have outgrown. As a child, you passed on the shirts and shorts that were too small for the larger you. They were simply no longer useful once you outgrew them, so they were easy to let go of. We can choose to let go of our small, limiting ideas just as easily, when we realize that they no longer fit our empowered, expanded self.

*Exercise*

# What Is Important?

Pretend that you have just been told that you have a fatal disease and that you have five years to live. Write down what you would do. How would you spend your time?

Now pretend that you have only one year to live. What would you do?

Now you have only six months to live. What would you do?

Suppose you had only a single month.

Notice the shifts in how you choose to spend your time, especially in relation to making money.

*Exercise*

# Picture Messages

Sit in your favorite chair and relax. You may wish to put on some restful music. Now take paints, crayons, or magic markers and draw a picture that represents your relationship with money. You could also get a stack of old magazines, a pair of scissors, and paste, and make a collage. The artwork itself is not important. No one is going to judge the quality of the picture. It can be abstract or representational.

Write a paragraph that describes what the picture says to you.

# 3

# FALSE MONEY MYTHS

*The great enemy of truth is very often not the lie deliberate, contrived and dishonest, but the myth persistent, persuasive and realistic.*   —John F. Kennedy

*LIMITED:* Money makes the man.

*EMPOWERED:* I define who I am. The amount of money I have does not define my worth as a person.

*LESSON:* To break the hold money has over us, we must uncover the false myths that have been planted in our subconscious.

IN THE past, people "knew" that the world was flat. People "knew" that it was impossible for a heavier-than-air craft to fly. The validity of these beliefs was taken for granted. They controlled how people perceived the world, and these perceptions were reflected in actions.

We live in a sea of beliefs and assumptions that govern how we see the world. Implicit and unspoken, they subtly determine all aspects of our lives. When we act on the basis of these beliefs, our actions are programmed by them and the results we obtain reflect them. As we objectify our thoughts through our actions, the outer world reflects our inner convictions, creating an experiential loop that is self-perpetuating and self-reinforcing. Only exceptional individuals can break out of these pervasive patterns.

But what if the core assumptions on which we base our actions are wrong? We create the world in our image whether our images are hopelessly distorted or pristinely accurate.

## How False Money Myths Work

Many convictions about money that are common in our society are as fallacious as the most ridiculous superstitions of our ancestors, yet most people accept them without question. These myths, widely assumed to be true, control how we perceive and relate to money.

For instance, many people "know" that if only they had more money, they would be happy. As they daydream about the changes they'd like to see in their lives, every image is linked to the thought, "If only I had the money." They believe that they must defer their satisfaction till that fabulous day arrives, and they cheat themselves of fulfillment in the present. Lack of money is their excuse for not being happy. As with any false myth, the penalties for organizing our lives around this kernel of "knowledge" are high.

Others believe a conflicting myth—that money corrupts. They hold themselves aloof from this dangerous substance, clinging to the imagined purity and superiority that comes with poverty.

Some people manage to believe both myths. They are drawn to money as a source of happiness yet repelled by it as a corrupting influence, and thus they lock themselves into a vicious Catch-22 that ensures the worst of both worlds.

I call these widespread assumptions about money the *false money myths*. They are held both consciously and unconsciously and are taught to us by our parents, teachers, friends, role models, and the entertainment media. These false money myths control our behavior without our realizing it. False money myths are not just personal beliefs; they are a fog that surrounds our whole society.

Our goal in this chapter is to learn to recognize the beliefs that control how we perceive money. By recognizing false money myths we take the first step to freeing ourselves from their influence.

## Uncovering Hidden Assumptions

Like the kittens who saw a world filled only with horizontal or vertical stripes, we are conditioned by the false money myths that we drank in as we grew up. Which of these five broad categories of money belief pull your strings?

Money brings happiness.
Money is the measure of self-worth.
Money corrupts.
Women don't understand money.
We have to fight for our share of a limited supply.

Chris and Cathy were an example of how false money myths control people's lives. Chris was twenty-nine and worked for a nonprofit organization. Brilliant, articulate, and capable, he passionately believed in his work. However, although he was doing executive-level tasks, he was making an entry-level salary because his organization had no money. One of his many responsibilities was to raise money for the organization. He had not been successful and the organization was having to find other means of raising funds.

Chris's parents had taught him the myth that money corrupts. They were judgmental of the few rich people in their town, who they felt were corrupt. Chris's dad hated Mr. Walsh, who owned the plant where he worked. Dad said that Walsh, like all rich men, cheated people and cared only about making money for himself. Again and again, he would denounce Walsh as an evil man who mistreated his employees. His anger broadened to include all rich people. It was the fault of the evil rich that the family was poor.

So Chris learned the false myths that money corrupts and that rich people are bad and should be disliked. There was no way his unconscious mind would let him have wealth and thereby become corrupted and hated. Even when he tried to raise funds for his environmental organization, which was clearly a worthy cause, his unconscious convictions blocked him. His conscious belief ("it's okay to have money for a worthy cause") was continually thwarted by his unconscious belief ("money equals exploitation").

Chris had been married for a year and a half to Cathy, when they began to disagree long, loudly, and often.

One of the reasons Cathy married Chris was that she admired his commitment to the environment. In this, he contrasted sharply with her father, who worked just for money. However, she gradually began complaining that they needed two cars and a decent apartment nearer to town. She was apprehensive about the future, since it was apparent that they would never have enough money for her to quit work for a few years to raise children. She was also upset because Chris and her parents disliked each other intensely. Her parents believed that Chris was a failure because he made so little money.

Consciously, Cathy believed that a person should work for a higher purpose and that it is important that love of money not control one's life. She came from a wealthy family that was unhappy. She consciously rejected marrying someone like her father. Her mother, alone and feeling unloved, spent her time buying bigger and better possessions, searching for the right house and the right country club.

Despite her conscious beliefs, Cathy unconsciously held to the false money myths that she was taught as a child. Her parents assumed that money was the source of happiness and the measure of self-worth. Therefore, unconsciously, she had feelings and doubts that agreed with their perception of Chris as a failure who could not give her a happy life.

Neither she nor Chris understood the dynamics destroying their marriage. Their web of learned perceptions and misconceptions about money threatened their whole life— and it was all below the surface. They saw the surface conflicts only—over childbearing, cars, jobs, and in-laws—and didn't realize that the invisible, underlying problem had to do with their attitudes toward money. Unless they recognized the false myths that were controlling them, Chris and Cathy were heading down the path to divorce.

Their way out was to become aware of the beliefs that underlay their values. Then they could take steps toward forming thoughts and beliefs they desire—beliefs that would serve them rather than hinder them.

Let's look more closely at the five basic forms false money myths take.

*False Money Myth #1:*

## Money Brings Happiness

The myth that money brings happiness is the most obvious and widely held of all. Common expressions that exemplify this belief are:

If only I had more money, I'd be happy.
Money talks.
You can't be too rich or too thin.
He who dies with the most toys, wins.
If only I could pay someone to do this.
Cash is king.
No one could live in a home that gorgeous and be unhappy.
If I had money, I could have him/her.
When I'm rich, I won't have to put up with this stuff.
He/she wouldn't be treating me like this if I had money.
If only I had a car like that.
When I make enough money, then I can do what I really want.
If I could win the lottery, all my problems would be solved.
Diamonds are a girl's best friend.

*False Money Myth #2:*

## Money Measures Self-Worth

Issues of self-worth are closely related to happiness, power, and status. Many of the expressions listed above reflect self-worth issues. Some additional ones are:

He doesn't have two dimes to rub together.
What a deadbeat!
She only loves him for his money.
It is easier to love a rich man than a poor one.
It's easy for her to say that—she has money.
Money makes the man.
Money is the measure of success.
Those bums on welfare . . .
They're only poor because they're not willing to work.
The privileged class . . .
If I lose my job, I'm dead.
I feel like people judge me according to the amount of
    money I have.
I feel guilty because I have more money than other people.

*False Money Myth #3:*

## Money Corrupts

Our society teaches in many subtle ways that we can have either principles or money, but not both. American movies and television reflect the content of our national subconscious, and one of the staples of modern plots is the conflict between money and integrity. The archetypal plot runs something like this:

A man (let us say, although it could as easily be a woman) is a junior executive in a large corporation. He is respected, successful, and making lots of money. His future with the company looks promising. Then he finds out about some enormous secret abuse by the corporation (the source of money). If he exposes the abuse, people's incomes could be put in danger and he could lose his job. He is on the horns of a dilemma, in which he can either close his eyes to the corruption, or face it—and accept the consequences. The choice is between money (or one of its surrogates—security, position, job, or career) and principles.

This idea that ideals and money are in opposite corners of the ring protrudes from the mass unconscious in many folk tales: "Robin Hood," "The Emperor's New Clothes," Dickens's *A Christmas Carol*. Even "Good King Wenceslaus," in which both rich and poor men are good, provides the exception which proves the rule. It ends with an admonition to the rich—"Be sure, wealth or rank possessing, [to] bless the poor"—implying that wealthy people usually act self-centeredly. The two protagonists in *A Christmas Carol* present classic characterizations of the two sides of the coin: either people are rich and corrupt like Ebenezer Scrooge, or poor and good like Bob Cratchet.

Having been brought up on these stories, we may find that the idea that money and corruption go hand in hand is implanted so deeply among our root assumptions that it is invisible to us. Many Americans feel a vague guilt about making money. Because we dare not do it ourselves, we are fascinated by people who unabashedly flaunt wealth—the movie star who spends ten million dollars renovating her home; the singer who publicizes a billion-dollar recording contract; the tycoon who names an airline after himself.

Our language contains many common expressions that exemplify the view that money corrupts:

Filthy rich.
She slept her way to the top.
Rich people are greedy.
The junk bond king.

He climbed up to that job on the corpses of his friends.
It's not whether you're right; it's how good a lawyer you
can afford.
She'd sell her mother for ten bucks.
I'll never sell out.
I wouldn't do it for love or money.
He sold his soul.
My family comes first, before money.
There are some things that money just can't buy.
That's a great idea, but can you take it to the bank?
Money is the root of all evil.
It is easier for a camel to go through the eye of a needle
than for a rich man to get into heaven.

*False Money Myth #4:*

## Women Don't Understand Money

The limiting myths about women, money, and power
have been examined and have changed greatly in the
United States in the past thirty years. For younger women
who are college graduates, much of the old thinking is gone,
but traces remain.

I graduated from an outstanding university, Cornell, yet I
unthinkingly assumed that my education had qualified me
to be "a good wife and mother." I don't like to admit that I
bought such a limiting concept, but in the early 1960s many
people thought this way. Some women still see their opportunities as limited simply because they are women. And
some women still define themselves by the men in their
lives, and by the professions those men practice.

Today's woman can have a career, a family, and money,
or she can choose any combination of the three. Yet recent
studies suggest that there are many ways in which the old
stereotypes survive. Here are some phrases that exemplify
this myth:

Women don't understand money.
Men are supposed to take care of women.
Business and finance are men's work.
I'm just a housewife.
The job market is unfair.
They always pay us less.
A doctor's wife
The general's wife
Your job is to find a good man to take care of you.
Math is hard for women.
Women spend money rather than making it.
Women don't know how to make real money.
A woman shouldn't be too smart or she'll drive men
   away.
We have invited Jim Richards, the doctor; George
   Stein, the lawyer; and their wives.
Woman are so dull. All they talk about are the house
   and the kids.
Women can't compete in the old-boy network.
We invite Mr. and Mrs. Joseph Jordan. . .

*False Money Myth #5:*

## We Must Fight For Our Share

The fifth money myth derives from the scarcity principle, the idea that there is not enough and that we have to fight for our share of a limited pie. This leads to the conclusion that we must always compete. The annual U.S. budget farce—morality play and slapstick comedy rolled into one—is the national manifestation of our individual conviction that the pie is limited. If we take money from one slice—let us say, defense—we will have more for another slice, perhaps health care. The pie is of finite size, and if one slice gets bigger, another of necessity will shrink. So our national constituencies (the Secretary of Defense versus the

Secretary for Health and Human Services) compete for a larger share of the budget in the same way that individuals in an office (Nora versus Sandy for Teresa's old job) compete for money and prestige.

The scarcity myth runs from top to bottom of our society. We look at the homeless people shivering in the street and feel that this is somehow connected with the limousine driving by. One person is of necessity getting less because another is getting more.

Common expressions that reinforce beliefs in scarcity and competition are:

It's a dog-eat-dog world.
If I don't get him, he'll get me.
You have to fight to survive.
If you don't protect what is yours, you'll lose it.
It's either him or me.
Fight for your rights!
You have to step on people to get ahead.
A small group of people control all the money.
The squeaky wheel gets the grease.
It's a jungle out there.
Heads, I win, tails, you lose.
The world is not a friendly place.
Welcome to the real world.

## Deflating the Myths

Now: Why are these myths false? In each case, a little thought is all it takes to break the bubble of belief.

The first myth, that money brings happiness, is perhaps the easiest to dispel. Think of the miserable rich—royalty whose marriages crumble; tycoons whose children hate them; movie stars who resort to drugs to relieve stress. The opposite assertion, that money brings misery, is just as false, for one could as easily find examples of wealthy people who are perfectly content with life. The fact is, we make ourselves happy or unhappy, regardless how much money we have.

The myth that money brings self-worth is just as transparent. In fact, the reverse is more often true: people with a natural store of self-worth tend to attract money.

Does money corrupt? If that were so, then we would have a handy way to assess just how corrupt any given person is: simply look at his or her tax statement. In fact, we could in principle make an inventory of the entire population of the world, ranging everyone in degrees of corruptness according to his or her net worth. The absurdity of the enterprise, and therefore of the myth, is obvious.

The idea that women don't understand money is so clearly tied to patriarchal, male-chauvinist attitudes as to require little comment. Certainly, many men have done everything in their power to prevent the women in their lives from having the opportunity to understand money. But that says nothing about women's inherent capabilities. In fact, one could make the case that many women have a *more realistic* understanding of money than most men do: instead of seeing it as something to accumulate indefinitely for its own sake, they tend more often to see money as a useful means for facilitating the inherently worthwhile experiences of life.

Perhaps the hardest money myth to dispel is the last—that we must fight for our share of a limited pie. After all, it's easy to point to examples in which scarcity seems to demand competition. And yet, when we take a larger view, it becomes apparent that these situations have been deliberately cast in competitive terms, either by ourselves or by others. We could just as easily recast the apparent problem in win/win, cooperative terms.

Take the example of the Federal budget, already mentioned. If all concerned—the President, cabinet officials, Senators, and Representatives—are unreasonably selfish, then everyone loses in the end, because the national economy eventually disintegrates. If everyone cooperates, though, the economy grows stronger and everyone wins.

But is it unrealistic to think that people with differing interests will cooperate? No, it isn't. As Alfie Kohn has shown in his book *No Contest: The Case Against Competition,* competitiveness is not inherent in human nature; it is a learned and culturally acquired attitude.

If competition were demanded by scarcity, then we should expect people in "poor" cultures to have a dog-eat-dog attitude, but this is rarely the case. In fact, it is Americans, who live in one of the most abundant societies in the history of the world, who are the most competitive of the world's peoples. Indigenous peoples, before their cultures were affected by modern ones, knew that whenever there is a seeming shortage, the best path to survival is through sharing and cooperation. Their reasoning is simple: If our attitude is one of scarcity and competitiveness, we tend to waste our energies in trying to defeat our competitors instead of simply expressing and enhancing our own unique capacities for production or achievement.

In sum: Most situations of apparent scarcity are culturally engineered by our society's expectations and attitudes. Over all, there really is enough of everything to go around. But in isolated situations where there *is* a genuine, temporary shortage of some commodity—whether it be food, money, time, or anything else—the best way to remedy the lack is for all concerned to do their personal best and cooperate. Taking the stance of fighting for our share of a limited pie only contributes to the problem we are trying to solve.

The false money myths are so pervasive that it takes most people a while to realize that they aren't self-evident truths; then, people are usually shocked to discover how riddled their thinking and language are with these ideas.

If you still unconsciously believe these myths, then they are holding you back from the prosperity that is rightfully yours.

## Shoveling Money

Money, of course, is and does none of these things; it is simply a tool by means of which *people* do certain things. Tools are always designed for a particular use. The British economist Sir Ralph Hawtery says, "Money is one of those concepts which, like a teaspoon or an umbrella, but unlike an earthquake or a buttercup, are definable primarily by the use or purpose they serve."

The shovel is a tool most of us have some experience with. What happens when we substitute the word "shovel" for the word "money" in the statements above? Speak these sentences out loud, and notice both the logic (or illogic) implicit in each statement and the feeling it evokes.

*Shovels* bring happiness.

*Shovels* corrupt.

*Shovels* make the man.

*Shovels* are power.

*Shovels* are the root of all evil.

She only loves me for my *shovels*.

He would sell his soul for *shovels*.

If I only had more *shovels*, I would be happy.

If a woman is too good at making *shovels*, men won't be attracted to her.

The person with the most *shovels* wins.

I feel guilty because I have more *shovels* than other people.

Time is *shovels*.

I feel like people judge me according to the amount of *shovels* I have.

The more *shovels* you have the more people will like you.

*Shovels* are a girl's best friend.

People will even divulge the intimate details about their sex life before they will tell you how many *shovels* they have.

*Shovels* make the world go round.

When you feel controlled by money or the lack of money, restate the way you are thinking and feeling using the word *shovels*. It will relieve your seriousness about money. Once you've loosened up, observe yourself to notice what is going on.

## Observing Yourself

*The Witness catches us in the act, but gently, without reproach, so we can simply acknowledge our reactivity and begin to let it fall away, allowing our natural compassion to come more into play.*—Ram Dass and Paul Gorman, *How Can I Help?*

It is not until we put some distance between ourselves and our everyday lives that we can see what is really going on. A useful tool for escaping from the snares of conditioned perception is the practice of witnessing, or *observing ourselves*. We do this by stepping back from our emotional involvement in circumstances and noticing what is going on, without blame or criticism. Observing can make us aware of the beliefs that have been programmed into us, without reproach. It is a powerful way of observing the big picture from the twenty-fifth floor rather than marching mindlessly in the parade below. When we disassociate ourselves from our thoughts, emotions, actions, and possessions, we have the freedom to view ourselves with objectivity and clarity. The truth can set us free.

The neutral observer notices impartially, without judgment. The minute we judge, we are no longer impartial observers. The observer perceives without analysis, comparison, interpretation, or reaction. He or she is not committed to any outcome. As the *Tao Te Ching* says, "The truth waits for eyes unclouded by longing."

The observer functions like a management consultant, who brings a new perspective by viewing the situation from a detached point of view. From this vantage place, new possibilities are apparent that aren't seen by the participants in the drama. This technique enables you to be your own management consultant.

There are many specific measures for developing the ability to observe ourselves and increase our awareness, and we'll explore several throughout this book. The following are good ones to start with.

*Exercise*

## Mind Mapping

It is difficult to get a snapshot of what is happening in our unconscious minds. Throughout this book you will be using various techniques to uncover the hidden thoughts about money that are sabotaging you. If they are to be changed, they must first be identified. One way to let the contents of your unconscious mind flow out so that they can be identified is called *mind mapping*.

Get some paper and magic markers, put on some soothing music, and sit down on the floor or at a table or desk. Quiet your mind. Then think of an issue that is currently troubling you. Encapsulate it in a word or phrase, and write this expression in the center of the paper. Circle it.

What are some factors in your life that relate to this issue? As each thought occurs to you, draw a curved spoke issuing from the circle and write the word or phrase that encapsulates this associated idea. Give each new thought a new color. Use as many colors as you like, choosing ones that seem right for each subject. Limit each line, if you can, to three words. You may use pictures or symbols if you like.

The words you've written on spokes may call up their own associations; write these on lines that branch from the spokes. Your branches can have branches, and so on. Make connections between branches, and have as many sub-branches as necessary.

Let your ideas sprout freely in whatever direction they happen to go. Don't stop to evaluate them or critique the process; just continue until you've mapped all your thoughts that are directly or indirectly related to the issue at hand.

Below is an illustration of a mind map. (Remember, use colored magic markers.)

## HOW I SEE MYSELF

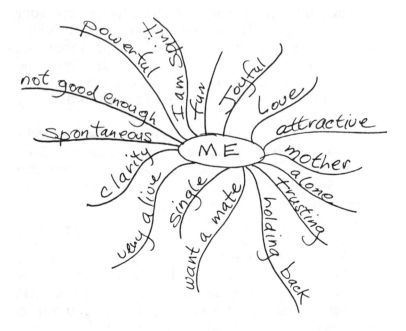

To start a money mind map, put a symbol for money or wealth in the center of your paper and circle it. Then draw a curved line out from the center and write whatever comes to mind. Again, map out as many related thoughts as occur to you, using colors that seem right and indicating connections between associated ideas. If you run out of paper start a new sheet.

Now write the word *power* in the center of a fresh sheet. Do a mind map on power.

You can make mind maps as often as you like. At first you will likely access the thoughts that are exerting an unconscious control over your conscious decisions. If you continue mind mapping, however, you may find that your thoughts begin to shift. You may notice that you are beginning to have more control over the direction of your thoughts. Mind mapping becomes an exercise not only for learning what unconscious programs are controlling your thinking, but also for establishing new directions in your life.

Keep your mind maps for future reference. Look at the example above and see how many similar sabotaging thoughts you have.

*Exercise*

## Observing Our Money Family History

Let's use the neutral-observer process to look at our relationship with money.

The first step to transforming our beliefs is to be honest about our present reality. As a first step to seeing where you stand with money, get out a pad and some paper and write the story of your relationship with money (or tell it to another person or speak it into a tape recorder). You can use the story of Chris and Cathy as a model. Tell your story dispassionately, as though you were an objective newspaper reporter with a simple job to do. Now, write some observations on the following questions:

1. How are you like your father in the way you relate to money? How are you different from him? Have you adopted any patterns that might have the purpose of proving that he is wrong?

2. What was your mother's relationship with money? Write down your mother's favorite sayings about money. How are you like your mother in the way you relate to money? How are you different? Do you have patterns that might have arisen from resistance to being like her?

3. Are there any rich relatives in the family? If so, what are or were they like? What did other family members think, say, and leave unsaid about these persons and their money?

People who do this exercise often have a powerful "Aha!" experience when they discover that they have been unconsciously stuck in a frustrating behavioral pattern simply in order to prove a parent wrong.

When Sarah did this exercise, she was shocked when she realized that her whole life pattern regarding money was controlled by what her father said about men and women. He was a general in the Army. He was strong and in charge. Sarah's mother saw herself as an unimportant appendage to her husband.

Sarah was told by her father that a woman could not make money and that her job was to find a good man to take care of her. Taking care of a woman was a man's job, according to him.

Sarah's father dominated her and her mother. Sarah resented this, but she was afraid to express her views and stand up to him. So, unconsciously, she set out to prove him wrong. She married two men who could not take care of her financially, and when I began working with her she was in the same pattern with a new boyfriend.

Between marriages, she tried to make a good living. But although Sarah is smart and capable, with a college degree, her varied attempts at careers were not successful. Her money history revealed to her that she was unconsciously proving one of her father's beliefs right and resisting the other.

I now realize that my being out on the courthouse steps bidding large sums for houses is a way for me to prove that I am different from my own father, who is timid and unsure of himself. However, by recognizing the source of my need to prove myself, I have freed myself from it. I choose occasionally to bid on real estate, but my primary activity has shifted to speaking, writing, and counseling, which I love to do.

*Exercise*

## Meeting Money and Power

Take out a pad of paper. Sit in a quiet, comfortable place. Meditate, or take a few minutes to relax. Give yourself as much time as you need to clear your mind and become still. Make sure you will not be disturbed, and that the surroundings are conducive to a quiet, inward experience.

Now imagine that money is in the room with you. Notice how you feel around money. With your dominant hand, write a message introducing yourself to money.

Now ask money a question. Shift to your nondominant hand and write down the answer that money gives. Ask money questions about its role in your life. Ask it about how you can change that relationship if you want to. Ask money if it has any information it wishes to share with you about money-history exercise you just completed. Ask money has any gifts it might like to give you. Once you feel that your interview with money is complete, thank money and allow it to leave the room. Be still for a few minutes, and appreciate the feelings that your encounter with money has left you with.

Now imagine that power has come into the room. Write a message introducing yourself to power. Ask power a question. With your nondominant hand, write down the answer that power gives. Ask as many questions as you like. Ask power if it has any observations or insights into your personal power history or that of your family. Allow power to give you any other messages or objects that it wishes to impart. When you feel that your interview with power is complete, thank power and allow it to leave. Spend a few minutes letting the feeling of the experience with power settle.

Write down how you picture the two figures that have come to you. Describe their dress and faces if you have a clear picture of them. Once you are done, look around the room carefully to orient yourself in time and space again. As you leave your interviews with money and power, remember that you take with you any knowledge or gifts they might have given you. Also remember that you can always come back and ask more questions, or get deeper explanations, at a later time.

*Training Our Mind:*

## Choosing Empowering Beliefs

Down the left-hand side of a fresh sheet of paper, list the limiting beliefs that came out on your mind map. If there are additional limiting beliefs from the *I can't because* exercise on page 24 of chapter 2, add them to the list.

Which limiting beliefs turned up in both places? Identify

the ones that seem to be the most problem, and put the most emphasis on them.

Consider the limiting beliefs you have listed. Across from each one, write an empowering belief that you would like to substitute for it.

LIMITING BELIEFS                    EMPOWERING BELIEFS

_____                    _____

_____                    _____

_____                    _____

_____                    _____

_____                    _____

Now let's use the NLP *Believe* Technique to help you make the substitution you desire. Start by adopting a neutral posture and transferring the limiting beliefs to the *doubt* side—the left side—of your brain. Next, take a deep breath and adopt the *believe* posture (see page 22). Now, one by one, take each of the empowering beliefs and place them in the *believe* side of your brain. Put your focus on the empowering side. You can also write the new beliefs in large print and put them up on the wall and/or make affirmations for them.

*Training Our Mind:*

## Changing the Intensity

We are going to add another element to the NLP *Believe* Technique introduced at the end of chapter 1. We are going to intensify the modality in which we experience our belief. First we need to determine how we represent things in our minds and how they affect us.

Close your eyes and think about friends or family whom

you love. Imagine an activity like a family dinner or party. What picture comes to mind? How bright is the picture? How large? Is it moving fast or slow? Do you hear sounds? How does it feel in your body? This is your *believe* mode. Some of us are visual and mainly see pictures. Some of us are auditory and focus on sound. Some people are kinesthetic and focus on feelings. Sometimes we are a combination. Just allow yourself to become conscious of how you experience things, so that you can use that information for your mind training.

Now imagine yourself winning a five-million-dollar lottery tomorrow. How does the picture look? Is it dull or a blur? Is it black and white or color? Is it hard to see? Is there any sound? Notice how your body feels when it doesn't believe the premise. This is your *doubt* mode.

The purpose of noticing the mode by which you experience your inner world is to enable you to use that mode to increase the imaginal intensity of what you choose to believe, and decrease it for what you are choosing to discard.

Suppose you had an internal-critic voice that said what mother used to say: "You don't know how to handle money." You could take that voice and make it fainter and fainter so you could hardly hear it. You could add static so it wasn't really understandable. Then on the *believe* side, you could turn up the volume on the new voice that says, "I can handle money." You could have the voice speak loudly and very clearly. You could use a certain tone of voice that has authority.

If you are visual you can intensify the brightness, enlarge the image, and add color and motion.

If you are kinesthetic you can intensify the feeling. Expand the feeling to take up more space. You can emphasize the *believe* body posture and concentrate on feeling it fully.

For example, I could take the belief that I am good enough to have wealth and put it in the *believe* side of my brain. I see it in large, bold, capital letters in bright colors. I hear my voice saying it to me in a strong, clear, determined tone. Then there is a triumphant burst of music and a "Hallelujah" chorus. I feel the sun shining, sending me rays in celebration. I feel expanded and joyful. I raise my head and straighten my back in a joyful acknowledgment of my worthiness and new-found wealth.

If you aren't sure which modality works best for you, use them all. It is fun to be creative and see what works. In the process, the right brain bypasses the left brain's analytical objections, so you are freeing a part of your brain to help you create the new reality.

You can apply this technique to the new beliefs and affirmations in all the following chapters.

# 4

## INNER POWER

*Oh, while I live, to be ruler of life, not a slave, to meet life as a powerful conqueror, and nothing exterior to me shall ever take command of me.*          —Walt Whitman

*A human being is not one thing among others; things determine each other, but man is ultimately self-determining. What he becomes within the limits of endowment and environment he has made out of himself.*
          —Victor Frankl, *Man's Search For Meaning*

*LIMITED:* I can't do anything about this. She did it to me and only she can change it.

*EMPOWERED:* I am responsible. I can accomplish what I set out to do.

*LESSON: We have the power to change our perception and experience of money and power.*

ONE OF the great illusions that we all labor under is the conviction that we see the world as it really is. We know that people have different worldviews, and that each person has unique abilities and habits of perception. Sometimes these come into conflict. We may theoretically acknowledge that people's cultural differences cause them to perceive reality differently. But when it comes right down to it, each of us tends to think that our version of reality is the accurate one.

And yet, our personal reality maps are largely conditioned by ideas about the world that we have inherited from parents, school, movies, advertising, and a hundred other sources.

Scientists, who are in the business of discovering what

reality "really" is, have this problem too. Old theories tend to accumulate, including ones that are only half-proved, and they all fit together to form a coherent view of the world. This coherent view is what scientists call a "paradigm"—a sort of meta-theory. Paradigms are unavoidable, but they lead to problems. Because they define the limits of reality itself, they tell us what experiments are worth doing or not worth doing, and which observations are "impossible" and therefore to be discarded. Our paradigm is our frame of reference, the lens through which we view the world. We organize what we see according to this underlying map of reality.

But paradigms change. People used to "know" that the earth was the center of the universe. When Galileo proposed that the sun was the center of the universe people were upset. He was seized by the Inquisition and forced to recant. The authorities saw any experience or theory that contradicted the geocentric paradigm as a threat. Paradigms control what our minds are allowed to see. We interpret experiences to fit our map, and so they "prove" that our map is true. All astronomical observations prior to Galileo's time were taken as proof of the prevailing paradigm; anomalies were discarded or simply not seen or believed. But once this paradigm shift had been made and the prevailing belief changed, the idea that the earth revolved around the sun seemed just as self-evident and reasonable to people as the idea of an earth-centered universe had been just a few decades earlier.

A paradigm shift has recently taken place in our collective view of communism. We used to see communism as a powerful threat, strong enough to destroy us. We felt we had constantly to protect ourselves and be on our guard. We feared our own citizens who had communist leanings, real or imagined. Our foreign policy strategists spoke of the "domino effect" in Indochina and Central America, believing that if one country fell to communism, its neighbors would surely follow.

But now, the old enemy has evaporated. The Soviet Union, communism's home, has collapsed. Our military strategists, some still seeing the world through the lens of the old paradigm, struggle to keep their balance by finding new enemies to justify continued lavish "defense" spending. Baffled, we try to make sense of the world the way it now is.

The Swiss watch industry went through a paradigm shift when confronted with the new quartz technology. In 1968 the Swiss were the undisputed leaders in producing quality watches. They had more than 65% of the market share, and 80% of the profits. In 1967, Swiss researchers had invented the electronic quartz watch. Swiss manufacturers, however, turned them away because the new watch did not fit into their paradigm of what a watch was—gears and bearings and mainsprings.

The Japanese held no such limiting concepts. Seiko enthusiastically embraced the new technology and began manufacturing electronic watches. Other companies followed suit. Japanese companies went from a 1% share of the watch market in 1968 to a 33% share of the market and profits in 1980, twelve years later. In the same period, the Swiss share of the market dropped to under 20%. 50,000 of Switzerland's 62,000 watchmakers lost their jobs. Failure to adopt emerging paradigms can be very painful in human terms.

## The Power of Paradigms

*These assumptions are the air we breathe, our familiar furniture. They are part of the culture. We are all but blind to them, yet they must give way to more fundamental perspectives if we are to discover what doesn't work and why. Like the koans Zen masters give their novices, most problems cannot be solved at the level at which they are asked. They must be reframed, put into a larger context. And unwarranted assumptions must be dropped.*—Marilyn Ferguson, *The Aquarian Conspiracy*

Many of the things we take for granted today, which seem so obvious as to be beyond discussion, will seem like incomprehensible superstition to our children. Our belief that human beings cannot travel at the speed of light, for instance, may be chuckled over by a future generation, just as we chuckle to learn that the President of the Royal Society presented irrefutable proof to the world's leading scientists in 1900 that it was mathematically impossible for a heavier-than-air machine to fly. Paradigms prevent us from seeing information that falls outside their scope. We mistake our mental maps for the real physical world.

The word *paradigm* comes from the Greek word *paradigma,* meaning "pattern." The word *paradigm* was first introduced in 1962 by Thomas Kuhn in his book, *The Structure of Scientific Revolutions.* A paradigm is a "taken for granted" set of assumptions about reality that controls how we see, believe, feel, experience, and act. This "reality map" supplies the outlines. We then proceed to fill in the details with our experiences. However, these outlines determine how and what we experience.

Look at the illustration on the next page. What do you see—a series of vases, or pairs of profiles? Neither interpretation is absolutely correct. What we see depends on which lens we are looking through—or, more accurately, which part of our brain: the part that wants or expects to see a vase, or the part that tends to see profiles. First we see one image, then in an instantaneous leap of perception we see another. This is the kind of dislocation of perception that Thomas Kuhn speaks of as a *paradigm shift.* Kuhn explains that gradually a number of experiences accumulate that do not fit the current model of reality. At a certain point, this body of experiences reaches a critical mass and we leap to a new

"Goblet Portraits" © Zeke Berman, 1978.
The Exploratorium, San Francisco's
Museum of Science and Human Perception.

paradigm, one that embraces and explains the previously mysterious phenomena. Every new scientific paradigm goes from ridicule to orthodoxy in a short period once this critical mass is reached. To illustrate such a shift in perception, read this paragraph out loud:

Now is the time for all

good men to come to the

the aid of their party.

If you are like most people you probably didn't notice that

it says "the the aid"—the word "the" is repeated. We make our perceptions fit our assumptions. In this example, we expect written words to follow certain accepted rules of grammar and syntax. When they diverge, we tend not to notice unless the discrepancies are brought forcibly to our attention. Proofreading is a difficult skill to master, since our brains tend to make everything look "right" according to our accepted paradigm of language.

As long as an assumption is unconscious, it is impossible for us to change it. Only when we begin to recognize our thought system does it become available to us, so that we can question and transform it. When we choose to change the map—our thought system—then and only then does the territory—the external situation "out there"—begin to look different. We can change things "out there" only by changing attitudes and beliefs "in here."

## The Limited-Power Paradigm

Our society is controlled by a paradigm that keeps us stuck in the same old patterns: We believe that we are controlled by other people, places, and things. This belief is another form of the false myth that the source of our power, happiness, and self-worth is external, tied up in an outside force called money.

Seeing people, events, or money as being in charge of our lives constitutes a major assumption. Most likely, the fact for us is that we experience life both ways, sometimes feeling in charge, and sometimes feeling controlled by something "out there." However, our society seems more supportive of the feeling or belief that something "out there" is controlling us. When we accept this assumption, we perceive our experiences according to this reality map.

We frequently hear in conversation how someone's boss *did it to* him, his spouse *did it to* him, the government *did it to* her, her friend *did it to* her. Such statements reflect a sense of powerlessness, of being the victim of others' actions. It takes a deliberate effort, or some kind of shock to the system, to break out of this kind of thinking.

In the summer of 1988 I had an experience that put me in touch with my inner power. I went on a firewalk. A number of my friends had done this and had felt empowered by the experience. I persuaded my college-aged son to join me. A friend of mine recommended Phoebe Reeves, who had learned firewalking in the Findhorn community, as a facilitator.

My son and I both had plenty of time to feel apprehensive during the hour-long drive to the firewalk site. It turned out to be a beautiful, open hillside. We shared the experience with about twenty-five people of varying ages. Phoebe was an attractive woman, about thirty years old. She seemed confident and knowledgeable. The first thing she did was to assure us that this was not about proving ourselves. We were instructed not to walk on the coals unless we got a positive signal from our inner guidance.

We watched a videotape that showed several different groups successfully firewalking. This gave us some grounds (not just intellectually, but viscerally) for believing that it was possible to walk across burning coals.

Our hosts built a huge fire, and we danced and sang around it. We each went up to the fire, threw in a pine cone, and told the group what it was that we were personally choosing to release and transform with the fire. Then, with another pine cone, we chose a planetary problem to be transformed.

Our instructor told us to remove all jewelry, as it could burn us. When I felt the intense heat from the burning coals, I could understand why.

Phoebe was the first to walk across. Several others followed. As my son approached the hot coals, I felt intense fear well up in my body. What if he got burned? He walked across with no ill effects. I felt a deep relief.

I asked my inner guidance if it was time for me to walk, and got a *yes.* I felt no fear. I walked across the coals several times. I actually bent down and picked up some of the glowing nuggets and played with them in my hands. Others did the same. One man walked across with his dog in his arms. The man who owned the property danced on the coals and rolled across them. No one was burned, though a few participants came away with small blisters.

I felt ecstatic that night and the next day. I had a deep sense of a new kind of inner power. I telephoned my friends and raved about my adventure. Six of them were inspired enough to join me the next month, when I repeated the experience.

One of the benefits of walking on burning coals is that in doing so we consciously confront beliefs of limitation. Parachuting, rappelling, wilderness camping, and other challenging experiences offer us similar feelings of empowerment. Once I had successfully walked across the burning coals and played with them in my hands, I strengthened my resolve to confront other beliefs. If I and the other people there, including my son, could do what was supposedly impossible, perhaps I could do other things that society said were impossible. The genie part of my mind took a step toward freedom from other limiting paradigms.

## Unconscious Reaction v. Conscious Choice

*Experience is not what happens to you. It is what you do with what happens to you.*—Aldous Huxley

People think events happen to them. In truth, events happen and we choose how to experience them. When we are reacting unconsciously, it does appear to us that the event is controlling us. People think that thoughts pop up over which we have no control. The truth is we can choose what we think. People think that emotions happen to them.

In truth, we choose how we feel: we choose to feel happy or depressed. People think that what they see is a fixed external reality. In truth, there are millions of stimuli bombarding our nervous systems every moment; we choose which ones we will perceive as reality. When eyewitnesses are asked to describe what they saw during an auto accident, their descriptions often differ substantially.

The truth is that our lives are determined far more by the contents of our minds than by external forces. We are bundles of conditioned reflexes. Our mental paradigms determine how we experience the events that occur, what we see, what we think, and what we feel. The actions we take in response to stimuli are the outward expression of the contents of our own minds. Our actions are the results of our preconceptions, not of impartial perceptions. Our actions spring from one of two causes:

1. Unconscious reaction based on old programming in our subconscious. In this case, we are not in charge. Our old tapes are in charge.

2. Conscious choice. We are aware and in charge. We can tap into higher wisdom. This is where the genie in our mind can work magic.

Whether we act consciously or unconsciously determines our power and wealth. We can react from unconscious programming or respond from conscious choice. When we choose actions that give us wealth, then we have wealth. To do this involves transforming sabotaging habits of perception into ones that routinely select wealth and inner power.

For example, if a person has a habit of thinking, "I can't handle new, scary tasks; I am afraid of failing," he will perceive a new job given to him by his boss as a threat and try to avoid it or escape responsibility. On the other hand, if a person sees the world from the perspective of "I succeed at most things; I love challenges," then he will perceive the new job offer as an opportunity to excel. The external event—the job—is the same. It is the person's perception that predisposes success or failure. Our habitual way of seeing the world forms the context that shapes how we perceive new experiences.

There are three stages of awareness:

1. Operating unconsciously.
2. Recognizing our patterns and habits and their effects; witnessing ourselves.
3. Consciously choosing our patterns and habits.

The outside world mirrors our inner world of thought. Wealth in the outside world comes from discovering our inner wealth. The direction of creation is from inner to outer.

We can train ourselves to become aware of what is going on in our minds. An illuminating question to ask yourself is: "Is this perception or action coming from my programmed reactions, or is it a conscious choice?" Once we have stepped back and assessed our options, we can make an intelligent choice about how to perceive the event, how to experience it, and how to respond.

## Empowering Ourselves

*Circumstances do not make the man, they reflect him.*—James Allen, *As a Man Thinketh*

If we have problems with lack of money, the solution comes from changing our paradigm of money and power. When we shift to the paradigm that we are in control no matter what, new avenues of action begin to open to us.

A middle-aged executive was fired from his job at National Cash Register. He had been found guilty of sabotaging competitors' sales efforts. However, an appeals court had agreed to hear his case. The word spread around his home town and Wall Street that he had been fired for incompetence. He was without a job for six months.

This man could have accepted his misfortunes as a defeat. He could have blamed his boss, his company, or his bad luck. His friends would have commiserated with him. He could have seen himself as the victim of circumstances.

Instead, this particular man saw himself as being in charge of his life. His personal paradigm supported his sense of inner power despite his grim external circumstances. He carried on, knowing that he had the power to change how he experienced whatever happened to him.

A company composed of three small, disorganized, unprofitable businesses that didn't seem to want to work together approached him with an offer to be general manager. The company's financial status was so bad that it only paid bills that were at least six months in arrears. This man agreed to take the job on the condition that he could have a stake in the company, sharing the profits as well as the risks.

His name was Thomas Watson, Sr. The company? IBM.

Like Tom Watson, we too can see ourselves as being in charge of external events. Eleanor Roosevelt observed, "No one can make me feel inferior without my consent." We have inner power when we know that we can decide how to experience what happens in our lives.

What we conceive of as being "possible" controls what happens to us. An ancient saying from the Hermetic mystery school summarizes this truth: "As above [in our minds], so below [in matter]."

The secret to empowering ourselves is to experience on the deepest level that we are *in charge of* the circumstances of our lives and not being *defined by* them. When we are self-empowered, we are open to new possibilities with respect to money, ourselves, and the world.

*Exercise*

# What Is Stopping You?

Take this opportunity for a little bit of self-reflection, and find out what you are giving power to in your life. Complete the following sentences:

The most important thing I would like to do is:

What is stopping me from doing this is:

Another important thing I would like to do is:

What is stopping me from doing this is:

A third important thing I would like to do is:

Here's what's stopping me:

What have you allowed to stop you from doing these important things? That's what you have given power to.

## What Stopped Me

My financial success came from a paradigm shift. When I was trying to make a living right after my divorce, I felt controlled by the outside world. My thought system was dominated by the "I can't" syndrome. Blocking my progress was a wall with a sign on it saying, "If only I had worked at a regular job earlier. If only I had gone to graduate school. If only I had more work experience. There isn't any way out of this predicament." When I began to experience myself as being the cause of what happened to me, my financial situation began to improve. I began to perceive myself, money, and the world differently. In Marcel Proust's words, I had "new eyes." The source of true power is within. Inner power and wealth are not goals to strive for. They are a way of being that we choose.

The word "empower" means "to give power to." The empowered approach consists of giving power to ourselves. It is a shift in the way we experience the world and what is possible. This approach is taught in business management classes using the term *proactive*. When we are proactive we are the source of action, initiating things, rather than simply responding to external stimuli. We are no longer *reactive*. Proactive people take responsibility for their lives and actions. The word *responsibility*, literally "response-ability," means the ability to choose one's response. In this state, our behavior comes from our decisions, not from automatic reactions to outer circumstances or people. When we take responsibility, we have choice and freedom. This expands our possibilities.

Responsibility gives us the power to change. We know that we can choose how we will respond to any situation. We see each mistake as a learning opportunity rather than a disaster that immobilizes us. The same outer event can have radically different outcomes for a proactive person and a reactive one. When we're in charge, we're not controlled by money, the boss, our ex-spouse, the weather, or a traffic ticket.

Victor Frankl, a Jewish psychiatrist, was imprisoned in a Nazi concentration camp in World War II. His wife, father, mother, and children died in detention. He witnessed and suffered unspeakable horrors.

Frankl tells of focusing his attention on his inner reality instead of the outer circumstances of his life. When he was working at hard labor, exhausted and hungry, he might nevertheless be feeling good, having a mental conversation with his beloved wife. He found in this most difficult of situations that "everything can be taken from a man but one thing: the last of human freedoms—to choose one's attitude in any given set of circumstances, to choose one's own way." He found that our inner decisions determine what kind of person we are in even the most extreme circumstances.

Frankl said he could tell that certain of his comrades would soon die if he witnessed a specific change in their mental attitude. When they gave up hope, when they lost their purpose for living, they died soon afterward. He wrote, "Fundamentally, therefore, any man can, even under such circumstances, decide what shall become of him—mentally and spiritually." Frankl chose to be self-aware and to decide how to experience his imprisonment. He was controlling his life on the inside, even though he had no control of the outer circumstances. He became an inspiration to the prisoners around him.

When we focus on the external factors, we feel helpless, immobilized, and victimized by the controllers "out there." Reactive language sounds like this:

I can't...

It's not my fault that...

It is impossible to...

They didn't...

They won't...

They aren't...

I have no choice.

If only...

I can't help...

Blaming outside sources turns us into puppets whose strings are pulled by money, job, boss, spouse, emotions, health, or the past. We then unconsciously set up experiences to prove our paradigm.

John owned two restaurants. He was always complaining that it was impossible to get a good person to manage the second restaurant. His underlying assumption was that no one was trustworthy enough to be given the responsibility of doing what he himself was doing so well. So he ran himself ragged managing both.

At a certain point he told me that he was about to hire his wife's cousin, Jeremy, to manage one of the establishments. I knew that Jeremy had a history of conflicts with people on the job. He had never lasted more than six months in any one place. John's wife spoke of how determined Jeremy was this time around to make a go of his life and his job. But in fact, there was no hard evidence that Jeremy had done any work to change his pattern.

I explained to John that if he hired Jeremy it would again prove his assumption that it was impossible to get a capable person to run the second restaurant. John's first task was to change his inner assumption that he could not have a quality manager. Then he could hire one.

The empowered approach is:

seeing,

thinking,

feeling,

believing, and

acting . . .

from the recognition that the source of power is within us.

Our goal is habitually to experience the world from the empowered perspective. This means retraining ourselves to *see* a different world. It means switching our lens, so as to experience the world from the perspective of personal power and choice. David Garth, in his book *The Power Is Within You*, says, "How we perceive power IS power." Examples of empowered thinking are:

Let's keep our options open.
Another possibility is . . .
Our choices are . . .
Are there any other things we can do to . . . ?
How can we include . . . ?
Some creative options are . . .
As a powerful person, I can . . .
Here is how I will view this experience: . . .
What I choose in this situation is . . .

The empowered attitude opens the door to experiencing our inner power when it comes to money—and everything else. This way of being attracts opportunities to us, and it gives us the vision to utilize them.

## Owning Your Inner Power

Inner power is not something "out there" that we have to pursue. It is not something we have to learn, strive for, gain, or accomplish. Inner power is within us, waiting to be tapped. Inner power is available to us as we erase the old tapes that sabotage us, that keep us dependent on outside sources, and that put us down and disempower us.

Liberating our inherent power is like peeling an onion to get to the core. It involves freeing the magic of who we truly are from the layers of erroneous programming that have imprisoned and immobilized us. Our inner power is in jail, waiting for us to free it and use it.

As we accept and appreciate ourselves, we open the gates to our inner power. We rediscover our own uniqueness. As our true nature unfolds like the petals of a lotus, we begin to know who we are and to love who we are. We begin to notice the difference between actions that spring from the tapes in our subconscious, and those that come from conscious choice connected to higher wisdom. As we notice the difference, we can choose to act from higher wisdom. We notice the feelings of harmony and peace that derive from inner power. We discover that outer power begins to appear, reflecting our inner power.

## How Do You See Power?

We have three options with regard to power:

1. We can be powerless.
2. We can have the traditional kind of power that comes from external sources of authority.
3. We can have inner power that is not dependent on anything external to ourselves.

Powerlessness is characterized by hopelessness and resignation. Powerlessness feels like a ball of soft putty. Powerlessness shows up in the "poor me" attitude of the typical "victim." We have all seen people who have given up, whether they're lifelong welfare recipients or society matrons who have stopped trying to find meaning in their lives.

A more subtle and socially acceptable way to be powerless is by outwardly trying, while inwardly sabotaging our own efforts. We all know people who are always trying to be successful, trying to find the perfect career, trying to attract the perfect mate—yet who never succeed. Success, happiness, or wealth is always just out of reach. They ride the merry-go-round, grabbing for the brass ring but never reaching it.

Joe graduated from Yale and earned an M.B.A. from the University of Virginia. He saw himself as becoming a high-level executive. After college he took a year off to "find himself," living near the beach in San Diego. The year stretched into eight years. He worked as a golf pro and occasionally gave small workshops on the self-help philosophy that he was studying.

Joe decided to move east and join the corporate world. He pictured himself with a $50,000- to $60,000-a-year job, like those his father had held, so he began to apply for that level position. His qualifications, however, were for a job slightly above entry level, more in the $30,000 range. Two years later, Joe is still looking—discouraged, and wondering what is wrong. He has set up an unrealistic goal and keeps himself powerless by trying to achieve it. His life seems pervaded by chronic anxiety.

## Power Outside = Striving To Obtain

Power that is dependent upon external sources is characterized by attitudes of striving, getting, and protecting. When people hold a paradigm that says the source of power is external, they have to work hard to get power. They have to be vigilant to keep it. Their power is dependent on the approval of others, or on the accumulation of money or possessions, or on other proofs of success. They are dependent on an outside source for their power the way an automobile is dependent upon gasoline to run. They have to guard their power from being usurped by others. Change is threatening because it threatens their power.

In this case, power is seen as power over others or power over circumstances. According to this standard, people judge whether others have more or less power than they themselves have. They feel separate from other people and from the environment. They feel the need to dominate. This kind of power is vertical and hierarchical.

In some respects, hierarchical power reached a kind of peak in feudal times, when each person was born into a rigid stratum of society that defined his power and status for life. He owed loyalty—"fealty"—to the person above him in rank, his lord. Lords owed fealty to barons, barons to dukes, and dukes to the king. This hierarchical model of power did not come to an end with the Middle Ages. We see it today in corporations and in governments, where power and authority is greatest at the top of the organizational pyramid and least at the bottom.

These structures assume a scarcity model: there is only so much power, and each person has to compete for her share of the pie. People have to strive, to work constantly to climb the corporate ladder, and then to protect their position from others seeking it. One person's gain is another's loss. Life is a win/lose, zero-sum game. The need to dominate and control others leads to manipulation, and so relationships become a dance of domination and submission. People suffer from chronic anxiety.

If one is good at the game of achieving external control, one may gain power in this sense. But this is no road to inner peace and happiness. Those who succeed best at this game have a high incidence of stress-related diseases and job burnout.

## Power Inside = We Have It Already

Inner power is a gift we give ourselves. We are not dependent on any person, place or thing for our sense of worth. The feelings associated with inner power are having, sharing, flowing, softness, and peace.

Inner power is neither hierarchical nor vertical; it is horizontal, and characterized by sharing, empowering, co-creating, and cooperating. It is not "power over" other people or the environment; instead it is "the power to." Your power is not threatening to me; rather, it further empowers me. We work together to empower each other. Inner power is not manipulating, dominating, emasculating, controlling, or corrupting. It is a team working together rather than a boss riding herd on the employees. Management styles that emphasize inner power, as used so successfully by Japanese businesses, are winning widespread acceptance elsewhere. In couples, too, the trend is towards partnerships rather than relationships based on domination and dep

When we have inner power, we don't *have to* yet we *are* strong. We aren't striving to get there, ⟩ᵤₜ ᵥᵥₑ ₐᵣₑ there. We don't have to get our needs met from outside; sufficiency springs from within our own being. We continue to grow, to accomplish new goals, but from a state of peace rather than one of anxiety and fear.

## Inner Power and Traditional Jobs

It is possible to function in a traditional job structure and still possess inner power. To an observer, the situation might initially look the same; but the person with inner power would *feel* differently about herself and her situation, and her choices and actions would eventually lead to a change in the situation itself. With inner power, anxiety is replaced by peacefulness. Striving is replaced by being. Separation is replaced by joining, sharing, and creating with others. Relationships are empowering, not dominating. We welcome change. Like the sun, we recognize ourselves as the source of unlimited energy.

*Exercise*

## Progressive Affirmations

Change in the outer world begins with change in our minds. Affirmations are positive, present-tense statements that we can use to change our own minds. They are best written down. Print them in different colors, so that your right brain can participate in the process of learning and believing them. I use magic markers, with different colors for each sentence. Make your affirmations short and easy to understand.

It is helpful to speak affirmations aloud. Saying them while looking in a mirror works well for many people. The best times to say them are before going to bed and upon getting up in the morning. Those are the times when the subconscious mind is most receptive.

If you resist believing an affirmation, set it aside for the time being and turn to a more modest statement that is acceptable to your subconscious mind. Then progress from there. It isn't helpful to mouth the words "I am going to make a million dollars next week" while your body and unconscious mind are saying "This is ridiculous." Start with statements that you can believe. Speak them and notice how you feel. If there is resistance, don't go on to the next step yet. For instance, in step 1 you might say, "I desire . . . " In step 2 you might progress to "I deserve . . . " Step 4 may be "I have . . . " If you don't feel your emotions and body in alignment with a statement, go back to the previous step and use that affirmation until you are ready to move on.

Write affirmations that fit your particular needs. From the examples below, use only what feels right. This is an exercise in tuning in to your inner self and in using your inner power to decide what works for you.

### Step 1
Use the words "I desire" to describe what you most want to do.

For example: I desire to be in charge of my life.

### Step 2
Say "I am willing" or "I deserve" to achieve those desires.

Example: I am willing to be in charge of my life.

### Step 3
Say "I choose," "I commit," or "I take a stand" with regard to what you want.

Example: I choose to be in charge of my life.

*Step 4*

Finally, use one of the following phrases to characterize your intent:

I can

I feel

I enjoy

I have

I am

Examples: I can be in charge of my life.

I feel in charge of my life.

I enjoy being in charge of my life.

I have inner power.

I am in charge of my life.

I am powerful.

Now go back to the things you found yourself giving power to in the previous exercise, on page 75. Look at your excuses for not being powerful. Craft an affirmation that deals with each of your fears. Keep your affirmations realistic, within the limits you know you can believe. Rewrite your affirmations until you know they are just right for you. Make sure they're short, direct, expressed in the present tense, positive, and reasonable.

In periods of rapid change such as our society is experiencing, inner power frees us to change. When the source of power is within, change isn't threatening. Free of anxiety, we can flow with change as nature does. We are content to allow the process to unfold.

*Training Our Mind:*

## The Inner-Power Anchor

Remember a time when you felt really in charge of your life; when you experienced yourself as the source of power, with dominance over all external circumstances; when you saw yourself as powerful and capable; when you heard the power of your voice. Step into that memory and fully experience it. Review the details of the event, seeing yourself there, hearing the sounds associated with it, and feeling the way you did then. Now make a fist with your left hand and maintain it while you are reexperiencing the event. This is called *anchoring* the experience. Release the fist as your thoughts return to your surroundings.

Now you can access this mental and feeling state by again making the fist. You can also strengthen the anchor by adding other experiences through which you are accessing and feeling your inner power. Tony Robbins has people anchor inner power when they are doing a firewalk. You can use any physical experience in which you call upon your courage and feel your inner power, or any experience in which you are in touch with yourself as the source of power. You can add new experiences as they happen, to reinforce and strengthen your anchor. You may want to use a phrase such as "I can do anything that I choose" or "I am powerful" with your anchor.

When you choose for something to happen and it happens almost magically, remember your choice, and anchor that feeling of "making it happen." Focus on all the times that you do experience yourself in charge of what happens in your life. What you focus upon will expand.

# 5

## HAPPINESS—GUARANTEED!

*People are about as happy as they decide to be.*
                              —Abraham Lincoln
*Money is a good servant and a bad master.*
                              —Francis Bacon
*Happiness cannot be had by any form of direct striving. Like your shadow, the more you chase it, the more it runs away.*          —Alan Watts, *The Meaning of Happiness*

*LIMITED:* If only I had more money, I would be happy.

*EMPOWERED:* I bring happiness to my life and money is my tool.

*LESSON:* We regain our inner power by recognizing that we, not money, are the source of our self-worth and happiness.

TO SUMMARIZE the relationship between money and happiness:

Money blocks happiness when:
- We are confused about what money is.
- We believe money is our master.
- Money is our goal.

We can have money and happiness when we have clarity that:
- Money is a neutral tool.
- Money is our servant.

Money blocks happiness when:

- We confuse money with our identity.
- We judge ourselves and others by money and possessions.
- We think money will bring self-worth, status, security,
and personal power.

We can have money and happiness when we have clarity
that:
- I know who I am.
- I accept who I am.
- I am not my money or my possessions.
- Self-esteem is how I feel about myself.
- Self-worth, status, security, and personal power come
from within.

Money blocks happiness when we use money:
- To "solve" our anxiety or fears.
- To separate ourselves from others.

We can have money and happiness when we use money:
- To love and support ourselves and others.
- To share with others.

Money blocks happiness when:
- We project our thoughts onto money.
- We forget that we give money its meaning.
- We see money as having the power over us.

We can have money and happiness when:
- We remember that money is a blank screen.
- We remember that we give money its power and
meaning.

Money is an abstraction—even when it is represented by
concrete materials such as gold or silver. It has no intrinsic
power. Its power is derived from the consensus belief,

shared by the whole of society, that it is valuable. It is this belief that gives money power.

The false myths that portray money as the source of happiness and self-worth are so prevalent in our society that they control our behavior without our knowing it. When we believe that any external cause is the source of our happiness or unhappiness, we are like the horse chasing the carrot dangling from a stick in front of him. No amount of effort gets us to that carrot.

Our society is stuck in a never-ending quest for more. If a thing is good, we assume that more of it is better. We are fixated on more economic growth, more housing, more security, more satisfaction, and a greater quality of life. And when we believe that money is the source of our happiness, then our natural goal in life is to have more money.

Illusion, when recognized for what it is, disappears. Our game plan is to become aware of the fallacy of money myths so that we may free ourselves from their unconscious influence. Freedom from illusion means neither chasing nor actively resisting. From this perspective we are able to design our life as we choose. Our goal is to be able to have—or not to have—wealth *by choice.* Then we can walk though the societal money-fog of illusion that surrounds us and know clearly that money is just our tool. We are free to live according to our highest purpose, allowing money to serve that purpose.

The truth is that *we* are the source of our happiness and self-worth. We bring happiness to our lives. We create our own self-worth by loving and accepting ourselves. Getting more and more money will never fill our inner needs. If we believe that it will, we are playing an unwinnable game.

I define happiness as feeling loved, complete, fulfilled, and at peace with oneself and the world. Happiness is a way of being, not a temporary response to a new acquisition or experience. We are the ones who bring this state of mind to our lives. No sum of money will do it.

The secret of happiness is choosing to be happy *now.* The

secret of self-worth is choosing to feel worthy *now.* Happiness is not a goal to be achieved by incremental degrees. Either we feel it now, or we don't. It is up to us.

When happiness is a destination, we are like wanderers in a desert, chasing mirages labeled "the right man," "the right job," "the right amount of wealth," only to find that they disappear ahead of us. There is always something else to be achieved, until we recognize that we are our own source of happiness. Realizing this makes us responsible and gives us ultimate power.

## The Lethal Cocktail:
## Mixing Money and Self-Worth

*Seek not outside yourself, for nothing can be found where it is not.*—A Course in Miracles

In 1982, a group of graduate students from the University of Duluth performed an experiment. They arranged for a car at an intersection to remain stationary when the light turned green. They timed how long it took for motorists behind the vehicle to start sounding their horns.

Their findings indicated that when the lead car was an old, battered vehicle, people began honking more quickly than when it was a late-model luxury car. Even unconscious behavior reveals that we habitually judge people by their appearance of wealth and economic status.

Money blocks happiness when we confuse money with our identity. Our language reinforces the underlying thoughts that "I am my money" and "I am my possessions" through expressions such as "You look like a million dollars" and "Can you take it to the bank?" From an early age we are unconsciously trained to notice who has the most, or the most expensive. We treat the bank teller differently from the president of the bank, the welfare recipient differently from the mayor.

Another study, reported in *American Psychologist* in 1978, had people asking for money for a pay phone. The same people were dressed in different clothes, to see whether people would respond primarily to sex, clothing, faces, race, regional accent, or other factors. The finding was that the single most important determinant in how often the supplicants were given money was the quality of their clothing.

We often find it difficult to be totally honest about money with others, because we are afraid that they will use the information to judge our identity and worth as persons. An acquaintance will likely tell you intimate details of his sex life before he will divulge how much he makes or what his net worth is. We seldom talk openly about money even with our children.

On the other hand, once the money taboo is breached, the subject becomes all-consuming. Couples sometimes fight about money in order to avoid discussing the real issues of feeling loved and appreciated. And divorce can degenerate into a mammoth money fight that only conceals emotional and self-worth issues.

Poverty has a distinctive mentality, just as wealth does. A belief that you are poor results in actions that confirm your belief. Many poor people actually say that money is not important, yet they have an anxiety about wealth that blocks its acquisition. They feel a resigned pessimism, a lack of initiative, extreme dependency, and apathy.

Being rich has its own set of identity and self-worth problems. Obie Benz, heir to a Delaware banking fortune, said, "Having money is like being a beautiful woman in a romantic novel: You are always wondering whether men are loving you for your body or your soul. You develop finely tuned antennae to detect whether somebody is being nice to you because he really likes you or because he wants you to give money to something. You distrust warm gestures and you look for their real intention."

Many people who have grown up rich take great pains to

hide the fact. One child made up a false address and never invited anyone to her home. Another made his chauffeur let him out a half mile from school so that he could walk like the rest of the children and no one would know how wealthy his family was.

Psychiatrists have even invented a special term, *affluenza*, for the problems of the rich. A significant number of sufferers of this malady lead lives of chronic anxiety, depression, and underachievement. As one wealthy man said, "You're not born with a spoon in the mouth that helps you cope with reality." Affluenza results from identification with money and from feelings of guilt. The children of the rich have often been chronically deprived of love. Their parents may have been too busy to spend time with them. They were given money or things instead of human contact. There may also have been a veil of secrecy about money, which led to the impression that money was dark and shameful, not something to be open and honest about.

When our identity is confused with our money and possessions, then the possibility of losing our wealth becomes deadly serious. Losing money means losing self—a frightening prospect. People who suffer from this confusion of identity fret about changing economic conditions, watch the stock market indices nervously, and elevate *The Wall Street Journal* to the status of scripture.

The reality is that security comes from within ourselves, not from accumulating money. Henry Ford said, "If money is your hope for independence you will never have it. The only real security that a man can have in this world is a reserve of knowledge, experience, and ability."

The reason that the psychology of money seems complex is that money is a projection of our personal identity, power, and status. Our society simply does not treat money as a neutral tool.

The way out of the fog of false money myths is to separate our identity from our money. When we are comfort-

able with ourselves for who we are, without ref
money, our sense of achievement, fulfillment, an
ing can be neither bought nor inherited. Our sel
comes from feeling good about ourselves. We are comfortable with other people, no matter how much money they
have. Money is no longer the yardstick for judging ourselves
and others. Our identity is not threatened when our financial position changes.

## Money, the Magic Mirror

In my real estate business, I often hear horror stories from
people who own rental property. They tell of tenants who
destroyed their apartments, of tenants who never paid the
rent, of tenants that began calling their landlords at home
every night. A wealth of such stories has led me to believe
that being a landlord can be either a horrible problem or a
joyful experience, depending on your perception. We attract
either positive or negative experiences into our lives in order to prove that our inner map of reality is right.

I have owned up to five rental condos and houses at a
time, and I've found the experience hassle-free. Occasionally there is a problem, but I have been able to solve each
one quickly and easily. However, my expectation is that tenants will love the property and take care of it as they would
their own. When I rent a property, I have an open house, so
I can meet and talk to prospective renters. I find people who
like to fix up and maintain their homes, and I give them a
small break on the rent in exchange for doing any required
fix-up and maintenance. I pay for agreed-upon improve-
ments. My renters see the property as their own and take
good care of it. My yearly visits to my rental houses are to
acknowledge tenants for the work that they have done in
fixing up "their" homes.

Our external life is a screen on which we project our inner thoughts and feelings about the world. Money plays an

important role in this process of projection, by which we play out our inner dramas so that we can understand and witness them.

One such drama casts money as a mysterious and elusive substance, hard to figure out and hard to obtain. It is something bigger and vastly more powerful than oneself. This may figure into the script for the social activist, the welfare mother, or the "spiritual" person who disdains money. In another popular drama, money plays the role of a powerful, dark, evil substance.

Some popular dramas that feature money in a starring role are:

- Sole heir squanders family fortune.
- Poor girl pursues rich tycoon but finds happiness with the poor boy next door.
- Idealistic young politician is gradually corrupted by bribes from powerful special interests.
- Young entrepreneur fights his way from poverty to wealth.

Some roles that money may play in our internal dramas include:

... a force for control and manipulation.

... a playing field to prove one's mastery; a challenge; a fun, exciting game.

... a commodity to accumulate and show off.

... the wall that stops me from being able to do what I want.

... the magic key to status, happiness, love, and security.

... a reward I get for doing a good job.

... a reward from God for doing well.

... the secret shield or talisman to protect me from losing power, control, reputation, or love.

... a waterfall nearby, always available, always abundant,

a natural part of life; all I need to do is walk over with my bucket and get some whenever I want it.

. . . a sacred trust to be administered for the good of all.

*Exercise*

## The Money Dream

Sit down under a tree or in an easy chair in a quiet room. Allow yourself the luxury of daydreaming. Cast yourself as the lead in a series of dramas, in which money plays each of the above roles. Picture the lifestyle you would lead, the places you would live and visit, the people you would have around you, and the details of your life. Pay attention to the *feeling* quality of the experience. Then write down your experience with each way of relating to money. How did it feel?

*Exercise*

## Money Situations

Pretend that your father is a billionaire. You are turning twenty and are about to inherit your first five million. Describe how you would feel about money.

Now pretend you are the child of a welfare mother and you never have enough to eat, as the money always seems to run out. How do you feel about money?

Picture yourself without any money, living on a self-sufficient farm where all your basic needs are met. How do you see money?

## Projecting Our Internal Dramas

*Webster's Dictionary* defines *projection* as "the unconscious act or process of ascribing to others one's own ideas, impulses, or emotions."

Carl Jung first described the tendency of people to project their shadow traits—the dark side of their own personalities—onto others, and then to blame the other for those projected shortcomings. An example might be the TV evangelist who vehemently fights promiscuity and immorality in the sinful world "out there" while unable to come to terms with his own disowned desires, which he acts out in secret.

Often, the person we tend to criticize mirrors our own issues. A person who has an inner feeling of rejection frequently sees other people as constantly judging and criticizing him or her, while unable to acknowledge the judgment and criticism that resides within that person. We may suspect that we are indulging in projection if we are often noticing in others a particular nasty trait which we believe ourselves to be innocent of. The expression "It takes one to know one" is the motto of the projection-buster.

This projection mechanism also operates in our relationship to money. We project our inner feelings and beliefs onto an inert substance called money, and we then proceed to believe that money *causes* those feelings, *acts according to* our beliefs, and therefore has certain inherent powers and qualities. We shine our thoughts, beliefs, and fears onto the screen called the world—and then we forget that we wrote the movie script. We mistake the movie for reality.

It is through the process of projection that we create our own reality. Even physicists have come to acknowledge that the assumptions and projections that we inevitably use in the process of perception shape and color the reality we perceive. For example, light behaves as either waves or particles, depending on the kind of experiment we use to measure it. We can therefore construct one entirely self-consistent theory of light based on wave mechanics, and another based on particle mechanics. The two theories will be equally true and equally false. The proponents of the two respective theories could point to irrefutable evidence and could argue their cases with ironclad logic. They would fail to see the incompleteness of their own views until they changed their assumptions—if even only temporarily— and performed an experiment based on those altered assumptions. As physicist Fritjof Capra says in *The Tao of Physics*, "Modern physics has confirmed most dramatically one of the basic ideas of Eastern mysticism: that all the concepts we use to describe nature are limited, that they are not features of reality, as we tend to believe, but creations of the mind; parts of the map, not of the territory."

The supposed facts that we allow to run our lives are in many cases about as accurate as the old truths that "the world is flat" and "the earth is the center of the universe."

## Putting On a New Movie

*The way out of money-based anxiety is to shift our perception of money.* Just knowing that it lies in our power to shift our perception can empower us. When we are willing to question the truth of our inner reality map, we open ourselves to the possibility of wealth and inner power.

Questioning our view of what is real will involve giving up the necessity always to be right. This can be a major sacrifice, since many of us would let go of anything rather than admit to being wrong. Many marriages that end in divorce do so because the partners can't admit that they may have been wrong. They are unwilling to adjust their reality maps.

In our relationship with money we have no opponent. The only person keeping us stuck in our position relative to money and wealth is us. If we picture reality as fixed, we have no options. Only as we see external reality as flexible and responsive can we have choices. Understanding that the projection you see originated in your own mind gives you the power to change it.

Suppose you get up in the morning and feel depressed and drab. You look in the mirror and see yourself all dressed in gray. You want to change the way you look, so you take out a bright red sweater and put it on the mirror.

How many times have we tried to change the mirror without changing our projection? Then we use our failures as proof that we can't change our circumstances or ourselves. I have a friend, Jill, who described a typical interaction with her boss this way: "I tried, I really tried. I explained the situation to him in detail and showed him what wasn't working, and he responded just like he always does. I knew he would. It just doesn't matter what I do." Jill is good at putting the red sweater on the "boss" mirror. She perceives her boss as a fixed reality, and the pattern of their relationship doesn't change.

How we feel about our boss can be a reflection of how we feel about ourselves. When I felt really good about myself, my bosses were encouraging and supportive. When I was in a period of my life in which I felt victimized, my husband and my boss acted controlling and mean to me. They criticized everything I did. I hated it and I could find no quantity of red sweaters to put on them that was sufficient to change them.

I had a tenant who was not paying his rent. I had allowed him to rent the house without the usual one month's security deposit because I had been working on a rehabilitation project for homeless people and had become sensitized to how difficult it can be to save two months' rent. So I had made an exception for this man and his family. Soon my tenant had all kinds of stories as to why he couldn't pay the money. He had lost it. It had disappeared inexplicably.

I was upset and angry at him, and also at myself for having gotten into this situation. But as long as I saw myself as "right" and him as "wrong," there was no solution. Then I decided to shift my perception of the situation. I chose to open my mind and to ask to see the situation differently. I began to soften, as I felt his predicament. He was a good person who had a problem handling money. In this frame of mind, I had a talk with the man. During the conversation, the idea occurred to me to ask him if he wanted his employer to pay me the rent directly. He thought this was a great idea. He worked for a small company that valued him as an employee, and they agreed to the arrangement. As I write this, he and his family have been renting my house for several years.

During the process of separating from my husband it was very clear to me that he was wrong and I was right. However, I had seen the destruction that happens to families when opposing lawyers fight to establish their clients' rightness. I knew that I did not want to play that game. Yet I found myself getting locked into the classic oppositional stance: He wanted this thing and I wanted that thing, and he was being unreasonable.

I resolved to catch myself whenever I started thinking that I was being unfairly treated by my husband and that all he cared about was himself. I deliberately shifted my perception to see how hurt and scared he was too. I made the commitment to change my perception and keep changing it to stay with the overriding goal that we create a peaceful, loving divorce, without opposing lawyers.

When he seemed to attack me or to be unreasonable, I forced myself to go inside to his pain and to soften my attitude so that we could look at the situation from a "we" perspective rather than the standpoint of "me versus you." Instead of trying to change my husband's mirroring of my perception of him, I went inside and changed my perception. When I did this, he would soften his intractable stand and we would come up with a whole new way of dividing things up. We both won. We achieved inner peace and learned valuable lessons, and our children didn't have to suffer the pain of witnessing their parents fight. This was a much more pleasant movie than the one I had been projecting earlier; I lost nothing except my inaccurate self-perceptions.

*Exercise*

## The Self-Empowerment Exercise

This exercise was developed by Arnold Patent to help people re-perceive problems. It is taken from his book, *Money and Beyond.* Patent has people use this exercise in workshops and support groups. I have experienced its effectiveness whether used alone or with others. If you are doing the exercise alone you can write out the instructions or speak them into a tape recorder before you begin.

1. Describe the situation in as few words as you need.
2. Close your eyes and focus your awareness on how you are feeling . . . Can you feel the feeling? Can you feel the energy, the vibration, in the feeling?
3. Are you willing to stay with the feeling and to allow it to be just the way it is ?
4. Are you willing to receive support in feeling love for the feeling? Can you feel the support coming in?
5. Are you willing to accept the purposefulness of this situation, even if you don't understand what the purpose is at this time?
6. If there is someone else or others involved in the situation, can you accept that you attracted them to support you in reclaiming your power?
7. Take a moment and allow yourself to perceive the same situation differently. Let another interpretation come to you . . . If you wish, you can share your insight.
8. Can you see and feel the perfection of what is just the way it is?
9. Go behind the apparent circumstances of the situation and feel the love in yourself and in all others involved in the situation.
10. Allow your heart to open and this feeling of love to expand . . . When the love has expanded sufficiently, let it

embrace the situation and all those involved in the situation, including yourself.

11. Feel love for yourself feeling all that love, and all the power contained in that love . . . Feel that power as your own.

*Exercise*

## Money Mirror Dialogue

Sit down with paper and a pen or magic markers. We are going to have a dialogue with money. Remembering that money is a mirror and that our most challenging experiences are the ones we can learn the most from, we are going to ask money what life's lesson is for us. You may use my questions or ones of your own that fit your experience. You can start with a recent experience or ask about an ongoing pattern that you have noticed. You may ask about anything you want, with any level of detail that you want. If something is not clear, ask for more explanation.

Write the questions with your normal writing hand, the dominant hand. Then switch to the nondominant hand to record the answers that money gives to you. You may also wish to use a different color of magic marker for each hand. After you write each question, close your eyes, relax, and let the answer flow in. Write down whatever flows in, even if it sounds weird. Send your internal analyzer and judge out to lunch and accept whatever comes. This is a right-brain exercise, and it is important to be completely nonjudgmental. After you are finished you can let the analyzer and the judge back in to comment.

Relax. Meditate or listen to quiet music or be with nature for a while. Now, with your dominant hand, describe a recent experience with money, or a pattern in relation to money. One at a time, write each question you wish to consider; then be quiet and let the answer flow in.

Money, what is the message you have for me?

Money, what is my role in this experience?

Money, what is it about me that you are mirroring?

Money, what can I learn from this?

Money, are there other lessons for me to learn from you?

Money, tell me how can I cooperate with you.

Money, do you have advice on how I can act differently next time?

This is an exercise to come back to whenever you have a burning question that involves money, or whenever an old feeling or habit pattern comes up. Make money into a resource and friend that you can turn to for answers.

This exercise also works well asking questions of power, time, or any other issue.

*Exercise*

## Happiness Affirmations

The affirmations below remind you to reclaim your power as the originator of your happiness and self-worth. They are particularly effective when spoken while looking into a mirror.

I am the source of my happiness.

I am the source of my self-worth.

I am the source of my identity.

I choose to feel happy.

Once we learn that happiness is a gift we give ourselves, we are free from the illusion that we need to be anything, do anything, or possess anything to obtain it. We are free to create our own personal image of ourselves as happy and fulfilled, regardless of our backgrounds or childhood programming. If you want a guarantee of happiness in life, the only person you need to ask is yourself!

# 6

## SPIRIT, PURPOSE, AND SUCCESS

*Worldly wealth [is] but a reflection of the real, the spiritual
riches that must be sought first, last and always. Having
found the riches of heaven, you cannot escape the riches of
earth unless you purposely repudiate them.*
 —Annie Rix Militz, *Both Riches and Honor*

*LIMITED:* I'll never have any money because I refuse to
sell out.

*EMPOWERED:* I can be true to my purpose and financially successful.

*LESSON:* Money is a neutral force. The way we perceive
and use money makes it good or bad.

ONE EVENING I was having dinner with a friend at a buffet restaurant. The main serving area contained a wide variety of foods, but most of them were not very appealing. They
were fried, boiled, fattening, and generally unappetizing.
Nothing before us was fresh, steamed, or raw. It was hard to
make choices. We debated the options and none of them
looked very good. We eventually filled our plates with the
least unattractive foods.

As we were walking back to our table, I bumped into another table that neither of us had noticed. It contained sal-
ads, fresh fruit, fish, and cold dishes. We had been so locked
into the problems that the main buffet presented us that we
had missed what we really wanted.

The either/or perspective is like that. It keeps you locked
into a limited frame of reference, preventing you from seeing a wide variety of alternatives.

## Seeing Both/And Instead of Either/Or

*Relativity and quantum theory agree in that they both imply the need to look on the world as an 'undivided whole'...*
—David Bohm, *Wholeness and the Implicate Order*

*Be in truth eternal, beyond earthly opposites.*—Krishna,
*The Bhagavad Gita*

The perception of absolute, opposing concepts is deeply ingrained in our culture. Our language identifies things by distinguishing them from one another. Choosing one by definition means rejecting the other. Dualities such as right/wrong, either/or, good/bad, white/black, and a thousand more subtle ones condition our thinking and way of seeing the world. In this chapter, we highlight some of the differences between this dualistic either/or worldview and the inclusive both/and perspective, and we see how the both/and outlook can be a tool for producing money and abundance in our lives.

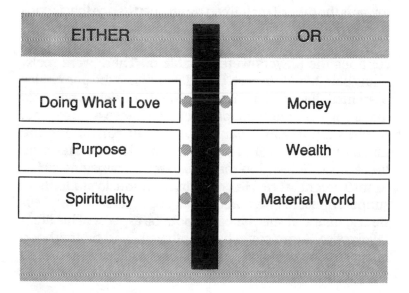

We appear to be faced with either/or choices often in life. Jerry, for instance, was a high-school student with a dilemma. He loved music. He composed music and had formed his own band four years previously. In his senior year, Jerry's father told him it was time to face the real world of making a living. His father wanted him to give up wasting his time on music and to study law, so that he could be financially secure.

Susan, thirty-two, was working as a successful stock broker. Her husband wanted her to quit work and start raising a family. She wanted children, too. But she couldn't picture herself just staying at home all day without the mental stimulation of working.

Such either/or choices are deceptive. The assumption of exclusivity limits the search for alternatives. If we choose a both/and approach, we see a world with many fluid possibilities. We interact with them in a dynamic flow. We can choose which possibility, and how much of it, we want in our lives. We can adjust and change with the flow of our lives, balancing sometimes towards one end, sometimes towards the other. Our life can be an open dance that is constantly re-creating itself to reflect our new perspectives.

In the above examples, the either/or lens limited the perceptions the players were capable of. There were really many possibilities in each situation, not just the one choice presented. If Jerry were a good enough musician, he could make a living at it. Perhaps he could choose a career that would support him financially without consuming too much time, so he could play music on the side. He could find a steady job within the music world, managing a club or instrument store. He could take on music students to support himself. There were really many alternatives. Music and financial success could both be aspects of his life.

Likewise, Susan could have both work and motherhood in her life. She could take a few of her best clients and work at home just ten hours a week. She could approach her boss about staying employed in his office, but with reduced responsibilities and hours. She could hire a baby-sitter for her times away. Her husband could cut down his working hours to spend one or two days a week with the children. There are many possibilities when we break out of the either/or mindset.

Our lives don't have to be made up of absolutes between which we must choose. We may believe that we understand this, but our thinking often betrays how deeply we are caught in this dualistic mindset without realizing it. The either/or approach is taught to us as children and often operates on the unconscious level.

## Having It All

The typical work portrait of a person employed by an idealistic nonprofit organization is that of a man or woman who works long hours in an understaffed, inadequate office for low pay. There is often an unstated assumption that working for a worthy cause is incompatible with making money. Even the term "nonprofit" defines the organization in terms of what it is not.

Jay Hair, President of the National Wildlife Federation, doesn't fit the above image. Other environmentalists sometimes voice suspicions of him for making too much money, for having too lavish a suite of offices, for being friends with people in industry. On the other hand, it is hard to deny his effectiveness, when the then Senate Majority Leader George Mitchell commented that Jay Hair was the only environmental leader that he was willing to meet with when drafting the Clean Air Act.

The interesting thing about Jay Hair is that he openly admits that he sees nothing incompatible between financial success and preserving the environment. His is the most entrepreneurial of the mainstream environmental groups, and it embodies the both/and approach. He proudly points out that they earn $30 million yearly from sales of T-shirts and calendars and another $35 million from their publications. Under Jay Hair's leadership, the National Wildlife Federation has become the largest environmental organization in the world, with almost six million members.

In our Western civilization, we have been looking at the world through a paradigm of separate, dualistic absolutes since the seventeenth century, when Descartes taught that mind and matter are two different realms. Only with the advent of quantum physics in this century has a new perspective, in which opposites are seen as complementary parts of one unified whole, been introduced into Western science.

Quantum physicists tell us that the underlying reality of life is a ceaseless flow of energy and that we impose our ideas on reality; they do not spring from reality itself. As we saw in Chapter 5, the long dispute over the nature of light was finally settled at the sub-atomic level, when it was discovered that light is both particles and waves, depending on how the experiment is set up. This illustrates how the universe affirms our perceptions of it.

Quantum physicist Neils Bohr clarified the disagreement between the particle and wave partisans by introducing the concept of complementarity. He explained that the particle and the wave are two complementary aspects of the same reality, and that each of them is partly correct and each is limited. Both are needed to give a full description of reality.

Complementarity has become an established way of understanding nature in atomic physics. Bohr has often suggested that we adopt this perspective in perceiving other parts of our lives. Psychologists and systems theorists have pointed out the dangers of divisive either/or thinking and the advantages of seeing the whole.

When Bohr was knighted in Denmark for his outstanding contributions to science, he chose as the motif for his new coat-of-arms the Chinese symbol of yin and yang, recognizing that his ideas paralleled this ancient wisdom.

As Lao-tzu taught 2,400 years ago, we can't have a negative polarity without a positive one. We can't have light without dark, or hot without cold. They are simply different aspects of one phenomenon. Heads and tails are two sides of one coin. Instead of denying or rejecting one in favor of the other, we should strive for a harmonious balance between the two.

When we see the whole, we recognize that wealth and spirituality are both part of the dance of the whole. They are complementary, intertwined. Only our perception has ever split them apart; and so our perception can put them back together. This shift in perception allows us to free ourselves from old conditioned patterns of judgment that focus on differences.

Applied to a relationship, complementarity means the ability to move flexibly between different roles, different aspects of our personalities. When I was married, I was the left-brained partner. I was the financial analyst, the researcher in our joint business projects. My husband was the creative one. Now alone, I have incorporated both aspects into myself. It is certainly not necessary to get divorced to shift into a both/and approach and discover different roles for and aspects of ourselves. Just knowing that it is possible enables us to make the shift.

Wealth and spirituality, power and spirituality, prosperity and spirituality—each pairing can be perceived as complementary aspects of the whole of life. In our jobs and organizations this awareness enables us to create together. In our relationships, we shift from me versus you to "we." In our lives and work, we create win/win solutions rather than win/lose situations.

My invitation to you in this chapter is to begin to notice the either/ors that may be keeping you stuck or limiting your possibilities, and shift them to both/ands. The following pairs of statements illustrate this shift in perspective.

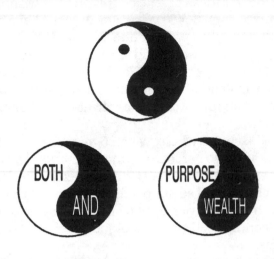

I can either work for a worthy cause or make a good living.

I can both work for a worthy cause and make a good living.

I can either spend time with my family or make money.
I can both spend time with my family and make money.

I can either pursue my spiritual path or sell out to money.
I can both pursue my spiritual path and have enough money to meet my needs.

List your either/or beliefs. Then rephrase each one into a both/and statement. The situation may not change before your very eyes, but as you change your beliefs, you open doors to new possibilities.

It is either _____ or _____

I can both _____ and _____

It is either _____ or _____

I can both _____ and _____

Now draw a circle for each both/and statement and put the two complementary elements within the circle as I did in the illustration. Picture them overlapping. Draw in color and post the drawing where you will see it often.

## Either/Ors—A Case Study

When David Wickenden graduated from college, he was inspired to live in the international spiritual community of Auroville, which had been founded in 1968 in Tamil Nadu, South India, by the spiritual leader Sri Aurobindo. Although Auroville was started by a Hindu yogi, it was open to all who aspired to its purpose. There was an atmosphere of universal spirituality that left each person free to pursue his or her own path. David's aspiration was to live a life that was based on his spiritual beliefs, and yet grounded in the everyday material world.

When David arrived in Auroville in 1975, he encountered enormous challenges. He found a community of 800 people from twenty-seven countries. It was built on fifty square miles of an eroded plateau that was no longer capable of sustaining life. Just to begin reclaiming the local ecosystem, Auroville had to plant over three million trees.

Since Auroville was a new community and had no consensus regarding basic economic structures, there were endless discussions about the relationship of spirituality and money. Some people felt that there should be no money changing hands internally in the community. However, the community needed to grow, and money facilitates growth.

There were purists who argued that they were not there to create businesses that made money. The assumption was that either they could be spiritual, or they could be involved with money. David called this the old-consciousness approach, falsely identifying things as either sacred or profane. Others argued that since what Auroville was doing served a divine purpose, the planet should support it financially. This is a classic mindset seen so often in nonprofit groups—that the world owes them a living because they are doing good.

David and others took the position that all of life is part of the divine. They argued that money is energy, a reflection of divine energy. They agreed that money had been corrupted by the way people used it, but they believed that, in itself, money was not intrinsically bad. Like a river that may flood, or that may be channeled to irrigate the land, it was a neutral force. They sought a relationship with the material world that would bring in financial support for their visions. If Auroville existed only in the spiritual realm, receiving donations from outside, there would be no connection with the material world and therefore no transformation of the material world. Auroville needed to use existing financial structures, but to do it in a new way and with a new consciousness.

Auroville was very much a part of India. There were four or five rural villages located on the plateau inside the boundaries of Auroville. David found himself in many dealings with the Indian government as he worked with grant applications and publications. Being in intimate touch with India's poverty, he began to look at the culture's thought system. At least one source of history claimed there had been a time when Indian spirituality had been integrated with the material world. However, for hundreds of years there had been a split between the two. The culture now considered the material world undivine and withdrew from it increasingly. As David explains, referring to systems theory, when humans withdraw their mental connection and energy from a system, it brings about the collapse of the system.

If one accepts the fact that there is a connection between how one thinks about things and what is created in the outside world, then there is a direct link between the collapse of reverence for the material in India and the rise of terrible poverty and human degradation there. India is a gigantic experiment in the power of projection.

There was a time when David didn't have enough money to buy a needed pair of sandals. He noticed that the external deprivation of material things began to cause an internal deprivation of his energy and spirit.

David articulately argues that if we believe that the world is a complete whole where all is divine, then our task is one of finding a way to see the material universe as an expression of the divine and to recognize that those things that have become distorted or corrupted need simply to be reclaimed.

Coming back to America after eight years' absence, David found that he had a greater appreciation for Western culture's success in harnessing the forces of material energy. He saw the expression of physical and material beauty as an expression of a divine quality. He acknowledged that America had created some ugly and corrupted expressions of material energy, but it had also given birth to much that is beautiful and elegant. People can create a beautiful and elegant environment only by energizing the stuff of material existence. And the only way they can do that is through the energy of money.

## The Love of Money

*The love of money is the root of all evil.*—Timothy 6:10

The Biblical passage above is often misquoted as "Money is the root of all evil." Herein lies the source of a web of confusion that has surrounded our society. We have confused the attitude we have toward money with money itself.

The fear of selling out to money and becoming a "bad" person—and thus losing our spiritual or religious purity—is deeply ingrained in the shared consciousness of our society. We have been taught by our false myths that money corrupts. We have also been taught that power corrupts, and that money is power.

Many of us have been given strong teachings on this subject by our parents and churches. The devil is often portrayed as using money or possessions to induce people to leave God. Most of us have heard the story of Faust selling his soul to the devil. Naturally, none of us wants to feel that we are selling our soul.

Even when we consciously see the difference between money and the love of money, our unconscious mind may still believe that money itself is the villain. This message may be on old tapes playing away in our mind while we are not even aware of it. When our subconscious mind "knows" that if we have money it will ruin us, it controls our perception and actions so as to protect us from the harm of having money.

Money as master most certainly can corrupt. Our society is full of examples of people who have corrupted themselves through their love of money, power, and possessions. The 1980s, sometimes referred to as the decade of greed, brought us stories of the rise and fall of the fabulously wealthy. We had the Hunt brothers with the silver scandal; Ivan Boesky with the securities fraud; Michael Milken, the junk-bond king; and Leona Helmsley committing tax fraud. Movies and literature such as *Wall Street* and *The Bonfire of the Vanities* reflected the same theme. The motif of greed coming before a fall is powerful in the mass subconscious, and our fascination with it drives these stories into the headlines.

History abounds with examples of the love of money and power destroying empires. Time and again civilizations rise to power, get too greedy, conquer other peoples, and then fall. Even fairy tales teach us this lesson. Remember King Midas, who, after his food and his beloved daughter had been changed into gold, had to ask the gods to rescind his wish that everything he touched turn to gold.

## Religion's Teachings

*Beloved, I wish above all things that thou mayest prosper.*—The Bible

Many people trace their beliefs that money is evil to teachings received from church. Throughout history the church has promoted poverty as a path to holiness. This teaching has been a powerful weapon for maintaining dominance over the faithful. In the Middle Ages, in alliance with feudal lords, the Christian church preached the virtues of poverty. The Russian Orthodox church and the Tsarist aristocracy forged an unholy alliance of wealth and privilege which endured into the twentieth century. The Russian Orthodox church's identification solely with the interests of the rich, and its disregard for the desperate poverty of the peasants, helped fuel the communist revolution.

However, in their original form, many philosophical and religious systems included the idea of fulfillment and natural abundance. The source of this abundance was seen as lying within each person. The Mystery Schools of Asia, Egypt, Persia, and Greece taught this knowledge. It is seen in the Hebrew Qabbalah, Hindu and Buddhist mysticism, and the gnostic writings of early Christianity.

In A.D. 180, Irenaeus, Bishop of Lyons, attacked mystical teachings supporting the idea that people could experience personal union with God. He was concerned with strengthening the power of the church and the priests. He embodied this point of view, common to the early church fathers, in his *Five Books Against Heresies*, which directed church opinion toward the belief that power and authority did not spring from within each individual, but derived from outside dogma, authority, and priestly succession. In 395 the Emperor Theodosius made Christianity the sole official religion of the Roman Empire, and the external institution of the church became *the* religious authority.

The intolerance of some of today's Christian fundamentalists is a pale reflection of the intolerance of the early church toward people whose beliefs were not in accord with official teachings. Those labeled heretics by the established church were often ostracized, shunned, discriminated against legally, physically tortured, and even slaughtered wholesale. The abuses of the church, when in alliance with power and wealth, were so evident to the founding fathers of the United States that they placed a clause in the Constitution specifically forbidding the establishment of an official church by Congress. One of the church's chief levers of control was the equation of poverty with spiritual purity.

Interestingly, most of the great men in the Bible either were prosperous or had access to riches when they needed them. Among these were Abraham, Jacob, Joseph, Moses, David, Solomon, Isaiah, Jeremiah, Nehemiah, and Elijah of the Old Testament; and Jesus and Paul of the New Testament. When Jesus needed to feed the multitudes with only a couple fishes and a few loaves of bread, He prayed and believed, and the loaves and fishes multiplied to an abundance, so that everyone was fed and there was food left over.

There are many passages in the Bible which clearly don't condemn money. John Randolph Price, author of *The Abundance Book*, collected these examples:

*The Lord is my shepherd, I shall not want.*—Psalms 23:1

*They shall prosper that love thee. Peace be within thy walls, and prosperity within thy palaces.*—Psalms 122:6, 7

*God is able to make all grace abound toward you: that ye, always having all-sufficiency in all things, may abound to every good work.*—II Corinthians 9:8

*Thou shalt remember the Lord thy God, for it is he that giveth thee power to get wealth.*—Deuteronomy 8:18

*Let the Lord be magnified, which hath pleasure in the prosperity of his servant.*—Psalms 35:27

Voluntary poverty is a valid spiritual path. Renunciates like Mahatma Gandhi and Mother Teresa have inspired millions. Celibacy, as practiced by certain religious disciplines, is also a spiritual path; however, most of us don't believe that being celibate is the *only* way to be spiritual. Likewise, renouncing wealth is not the *only* spiritual path. We can choose to be stewards of wealth in service to the planet. If all spiritual people were to reject wealth, then by default they would give the power of money to others who would spend it quite differently.

## Using Money as Love and Support

We can corrupt our lives when we use money:
To supposedly solve our anxiety or fears;
To separate ourselves from others.

We can have happiness when we use money:
To love and support ourselves and others;
To share with others.

Howard Hughes is an extreme example of how we can use money to hide fear and create separation. The fate of this billionaire refutes the popular myth that money brings happiness. He used money to build a wall between himself and the rest of humanity. No one was allowed to touch him, to call him on the telephone, or to initiate a visit or conversation with him. He was so afraid of germs that he made his secretaries and assistants wear white gloves and go through decontamination rituals. If he hadn't had money, he would have been forced to interact more with other people. During a scandal in the early 1950s, when he had to relate more to people for a while, his well-being improved. Greed and feelings of fear and separateness are mutually reinforcing.

Hughes's life is an extreme case of money-induced seclusion. However, in small ways many people use money subtly to separate themselves from others. Examples include the person who starts making a lot more money and drops his old friends, and the one who chases after people with money and secretly disdains acquaintances who have less.

Josephine was chronically lonely and depressed. She had inherited money and didn't have to work. She lived alone and spent a lot of time searching for the right psychiatrist or a new kind of healer. Then she read that giving money away cures depression. She started giving her money away, and her life began to change dramatically. She got involved in some of the organizations she was supporting. Her depression totally disappeared. She is now a vibrant community leader and activist, and she serves as president of a nonprofit organization she founded. Her enthusiasm and joy touch everyone she meets.

Sharing can be profitable. Sony, the electronics giant that developed Betamax videotape technology, didn't license their product to other manufacturers. Their rival, JVC, who developed the competing VHS model, shared their technical standards and manufacturing techniques with others. Even though most experts thought that Betamax was the better technology, the market share of Sony's Betamax shrank from the 100% it enjoyed in 1975 to only 28% in 1981. The VHS model, which became available with many varieties to choose from, became the de facto industry standard.

Martha started a real estate firm. She had a lot of contacts, which she willingly shared with her agents. When she got a client call she gave it to her sales people, happily sharing in their success. The word got around that hers was a great office to work in. Within a few years she had one of the largest and most prosperous real estate firms in town.

On the other hand, two brothers of my acquaintance opened a real estate firm and carefully guarded "their" clients. They felt it was up to their sales people to make their own contacts. If a prospect walked in off the street, one brother (the office manager) would direct the person to the other brother. Ten years later they are still complaining that it is impossible to find decent help.

When we share money, we also share a common bond. Back in the '80s, which the media declared the "Me Decade," a man called Joshua Mailman founded an organization called the Threshold Foundation, otherwise known as "the Donuts Network." In their words, "Our commitment is to healing, by listening to each other and to our higher selves, and extending this healing into the world in the deepest ways we can. Today, the earth's need to survive calls us to awaken to the divine within all creation."

The organization was first started for people who had inherited money, to encourage them to help each other deal with the special problems they face. Many such people tend to feel guilty and isolated. Many have experienced alcohol and drug addictions in their families. The Threshold Foundation has broadened to three hundred member-philanthropists, and it now includes people who have earned their wealth rather than inheriting it. Members empower each other by sharing their experiences of using money to be of service. They are committed to being wise stewards of wealth. They teach each other the joy of caring deeply for others and for the earth. The group raises and contributes about a million dollars each year to causes that they carefully select.

Scottish-born industrialist Andrew Carnegie gave away his money as he earned it, and it just kept coming in. He started his career at age twelve, working long hours as a bobbin boy. He went on to create 2,407 public libraries so that poor people could have access to books, which had been his own path from poverty to wealth. Carnegie demonstrated his love for others and for the world through his philanthropic activities. He exemplified both financial abundance and happiness. In his words, "Surplus wealth is a sacred trust which its possessor is bound to administer in his lifetime for the good of the community."

We don't have to have a large fortune or belong to any organization to find the joy of sharing with one another. And, of course, sharing doesn't have to involve money. The most meaningful sharing is the sharing of our time, our love, and our life, in whatever form is natural and helpful. Armand Hammer, chairman of Occidental Petroleum, said, "I have never prayed for power or fame or riches, though I have enjoyed them all in abundance. In all my time and all my actions, I have tried to accomplish something of lasting benefit to the world; to add what I can to the riches of the planet and to share with all people the beauty and the delight of life."

## Trusting Ourselves to Use Money Rightly

*In God We Trust*—On the U.S. one-dollar bill

Fear of misusing money is a major block to allowing money to flow into our lives. When our founding fathers put In God We Trust on their coinage, they were giving us very good advice. The feeling of trusting God, or the divine force in ourselves, to use money rightly is the secret to allowing it to flow in without fear of corruption.

When we know that our attitudes, not money, do the corrupting, we can trust ourselves to choose to use money rightly. Observing where our perceptions are coming from—from fear-anxiety, or love-trust—will make it clear what action to choose. We can choose to be guided by our aware observer, grounded in clarity and love, and in doing so we will use money rightly regardless of the circumstance.

Often spiritual people and social activists are afraid that they might misuse wealth, so they avoid it. But this avoidance could be seen as a subtle abdication of responsibility. When we avoid wealth we give away the power to decide how the resources of the planet are to be used. Whenever I have clients who are committed to a vision for the planet but blocking out the money to support it, I remind them that being poor can be selfish.

Remember the metaphor of the empty water pitcher, the half-full pitcher and the ever-filled pitcher? When we let go of our blocks and fears and allow our pitcher to be full, we can share. It is a path of service to be willing to be a steward of money and to use it in ways that will serve humanity.

This is not the path for everyone. Nuns and monks have chosen a different path of service. However, this planet needs some spiritual stewards to redirect how we use our resources and wealth. A planet that is abundant and sharing can support a more harmonious quality of life. The Garden of Eden was not a garden of lack.

In the myth of the hero's journey, the hero readily accepts the tools that allow him to perform his heroic act. Being a steward of money power in the world can be seen as a modern hero's journey. My invitation to you is to accept the tools of wealth and power that enable you to achieve your vision.

If it feels appropriate, you can personally *redefine money* in your mind to be an extension of the universal God-energy flowing through you. Your job is to channel money into the physical plane so that it can be used in a way that supports you and others. From the spiritual point of view, money is the physical aspect of the spiritual wealth of God.

As Eric Butterworth says in *Spiritual Politics,* "Money is God in action."

# 7

## ABUNDANCE: THE MAGIC OF ENOUGH

*He is rich who knows he has enough.*
— Lao-tzu, *The Tao Te Ching*

*LIMITED:* I feel anxious about not having enough.

*EMPOWERED:* I am peaceful; I feel that I have enough money and that I'll always have enough.

*LESSON:* I can choose abundance. I can choose to have enough, to be enough, and to feel the inner peace that comes from having enough.

WHO AMONG us has never complained that there's just not enough time? The lament is nearly universal. Ironically, even the national news magazine *Time* has added its voice to the chorus; in an article entitled "How America Has Run Out of Time," it was noted that "Workers are weary, parents are frantic and even children haven't a moment to spare."

The Hallmark Company, ever attuned to the mass psyche, has created a line of cards for parents who don't have time to see their children. There are cards for breakfast, wishing children a good day, and cards for under the pillow, wishing them a good night's sleep.

The reasons for our lack of time are many and deep; Jeremy Rifkin explored them brilliantly in his 1987 book *Time Wars*. But time is hardly the only commodity we're short on. Our society seems wedded to the assumption that we don't have enough time, enough money, enough knowledge, or enough possessions. In virtually every field, we are constantly striving for *more*.

Businessmen have complained to me of the "more" syndrome in commerce. One friend told me that when a particularly good salesman in his company surprised everyone by hitting his quota, the company promptly increased the quota by 20%. He lamented that this sort of pressure was driving people crazy. Many were burning out.

Is this relentless quest for more necessary? Is it healthy? Is there an alternative?

## Striving, Striving: How Much is Enough?

*In order to feel real and well, he had to exceed himself constantly, make more money, build bigger buildings. Underneath there's despair: Nothing I do is enough, and it never will be.*—A colleague of Donald Trump, quoted in *Parade* magazine

The trouble with having more as our goal is that there is never an end in sight. We are forever chasing rainbows that are out of reach, no matter how far or how fast we run.

*The Wall Street Journal* described the Bush Administration as having more economic growth as its holy grail. Our economy is based on the conviction that more is better, and that growth must be constant and unending. We measure our national growth according to the Gross National Product, without regard to environmental destruction, human costs, or the quality of life. We assume that having more equals happiness, both for society and for the individual. It's no wonder that sociologists characterize America as "the acquisitive society."

The constant desire for more comes from a feeling of not having enough, which in turn derives from an underlying belief in scarcity—a conviction that we live in a world of limited supply and that we have to compete for our piece of the pie. This belief leads to driven, insecure, and anxious behavior.

The scarcity model was probably a part of our upbringing. Most of us didn't feel unconditionally loved by our parents. Love and approval were usually bestowed as a reward for doing the "right" thing. Our parents unconsciously sent us messages that said:

"Get better grades and Mommy and Daddy will be pleased and love you."

"Be a better baseball pitcher, tennis player, or gymnast, and we will love you."

"Be more popular and have more friends; that'll prove you're lovable."

"Fit in with the program and you'll get approval."

As a result, we (again, unconsciously) drew the inevitable conclusion that we were not good enough just as we were. That message was reinforced when we saw our parents expressing the same dissatisfaction with themselves and their circumstances, always striving to be better, with money as the single most important measure of what "better" meant.

This constant striving for more is a form of addiction. The concept of addiction was once seen as applying only to psychological and physical dependence on drugs and alcohol, but in recent years researchers have found that virtually any experience can be the object of an addiction. In essence, addiction is a pathological state of dependency on something external to meet unfilled inner needs. The addict uses his or her relationship with the object of addiction as a preoccupation with which to blot out feelings of inadequacy. Money and success can be objects of addiction, as can food, sex, and drugs. At least one successful twelve-step program, Debtors Anonymous, recognizes the addictive power of spending money and helps members become free of it.

Recovery from money addiction is made difficult by the fact that it is a form of dependency that is blessed and encouraged by our entire social structure. Yet whenever we use money as a screen with which to hide our fears and insecurities, the results are destructive to ourselves, our families, and our world. Every addiction masks unsatisfied inner needs, and until these needs are recognized and met we are on a merry-go-round of denial, deception, and acting out.

The results of money addiction (at least, when carried to extremes) are clear. The news media regularly feature stories of people who have managed to run up tens or hundreds of thousands of dollars in credit-card debt, while their income remained modest or nonexistent. Yet even the addict who is a spectacular financial "success" eventually leaves behind a trail of broken promises, suffering, and hardship. We all know the story of Donald Trump, the real estate king whose inflated ego (no doubt masking a deep-seated void) precipitated his own fall from the pinnacles of power. He had emblazoned his name on Trump Tower, Trump Plaza, Trump Parc, Trump Palace, Trump Castle, the Trump Princess yacht, Trump Shuttle, and the Trump Taj Mahal Casino. His goal was to own the biggest and the best, and to be sure that everyone knew about it.

Similar is the saga of Michael Milken, the junk-bond king, who likewise personified the mania for more. At the height of his influence, Milken made $1 billion over a four-year period, including $500 million in salary for 1987, which was the equivalent of $1.5 million a day and $107,000 an hour. After his conviction for fraud and insider trading, the fines and penalties levied against him totalled some $600 million. Michael Milken had produced nothing, invented nothing, manufactured nothing. He had made deals.

Just how much money is enough? The cover of an issue of *Parade* magazine featured a baseball pitcher who made $2.8 million and a C.E.O. who received $1.3 million. The United States now has fifty-five billionaires and Japan has forty-one. Obviously, a person with this much money has vastly more than enough to supply any conceivable physical need. In such a case, money has become an ego symbol, a way of sublimating drives that have nothing to do with food, shelter, or security.

In his book *Modern Madness*, psychiatrist Douglas LaBier

describes people he calls "troubled winners" and "the working wounded"—those who have found that their success at
work has led to emptiness and despair instead of happiness
and fulfillment. Psychologist Steven Berglas, author of *The
Success Syndrome, proposes that many of these driven rich*
"haven't really developed an ego or a sense of self-esteem."
Society and their parents rewarded them for achieving, and
so achievement has became their *only* route to love and acceptance. But using money to get love and acceptance leads
to irrational, addictive behavior.

## The Scarcity Attitude

Suzanne inherited several million dollars when her husband died. She was college-educated and had just turned
forty. To most people, her situation would seem to justify
sadness or grief, but hardly panic—which was her reaction.
She lived in a perpetual undercurrent of fear, constantly
counting her money and consulting financial advisors. She
was terrified of scarcity.

In contrast, another client had about $1,000 in the bank
when she lost her job. However, she was quite relaxed. Her
comment to me was: "I guess it's time for me to move into
the career I really want. I've been putting off making a decision, and now this pushes me into the new direction." The
fear of scarcity hardly entered her thinking.

Scarcity thinking bears little relation to our actual financial status. I have known millionaires who were very much
afraid that they didn't have enough. On the other hand, one
woman who grew up on a farm told me that she was
shocked when she learned that her parents' income was
below the official poverty level. She had never once felt poor.
There was always plenty to eat, and everyone in the family
trusted that there would always be enough.

A friend of mine believes in a scarcity of time. She is always frantically busy, yet always behind. Whenever I am

with her for a while, I find myself feeling hurried and anxious. I would never call her to share a personal triumph or problem unless I felt it was "important," for fear of bothering her. When I talk to her I make my conversations short so as not to "waste" her time. She usually comes late, leaves early, and often cancels her plans with me.

But another friend has an abundance of time. The more she shares, the more she seems to have. She has a powerful job and always seems to have everything well under control.

When we see the world as a place where we have to fight for our share, we separate ourselves from others. This leads to feelings of loneliness and fear. We externalize these inner states by putting burglar gates on our apartments, alarms on our cars, and cans of mace in our purses. On the national level, we distrust other nations and channel our resources into weapons of war.

The main source of the scarcity attitude is the belief in a self that is "not good enough," an image that was constructed for us during our upbringing. This inner lack shows up in our experience as a sense of outer scarcity.

The scarcity mental and emotional state is characterized by:

drivenness and anxiety
fear
the constant need for more
seeing few choices/possibilities
feeling pressured
believing there isn't enough
busyness
resistance to change
focusing on the past or future
hoarding

focusing on what is missing
feeling stuck
feeling separate and alone
frustration
attachment to the way things are
judgmentalism
addictive consumption
low self-esteem
greed

The abundance mental and emotional state is:

full of love
relaxed
trusting
natural and harmonious
peaceful
joyous
fun
assured that there is enough
cooperative
secure
sharing
grateful
happy
aware of many possibilities
focused on being

free
accepting of change
expansive
feeling part of the whole
a source of positive vision
creative
innovative
supportive
feeling connected to others
unattached to specific out-
    comes
flowing
giving and receiving
high in self-esteem

Money addiction and the scarcity attitude nearly always go together. That's because when we are convinced that there is never enough, money ceases to be a tool for the practical achievement of our life's purposes and becomes instead a drug to help stave off worry and depression. A healthy relationship with money begins with an attitude of abundance.

## Seeing Beyond the Appearance of Limitation

There is no greater example of the abundance attitude than the life and teachings of Jesus as reported in the Bible. He wasn't controlled by thoughts of lack and limitation. There are no stories of Him saying to His disciples, "We can't do this because we don't have enough money." Yet there were times when anyone else would have felt cause for complaint. In one instance, several thousand people gathered to hear Jesus teach. After three days had passed, they grew hungry—but no one had brought food. The disciples said to Jesus, "How can we find bread in the wilderness to feed a multitude? We have only seven loaves of bread and a few fishes."

Jesus said, "I will not send the people away weak from fasting." He took the food that was available and blessed it and asked for it to multiply. Instead of staying in the world's thought system, which saw an impossible lack, Jesus trusted and tuned in to the underlying world of thought wherein all is possible. He brought forth from the realm of unlimited abundance.

This story can be a powerful metaphor for our own lives. We can recognize what we have, bless it, give thanks for it, and believe and trust that abundance is available in the underlying world of thought.

The record of Jesus' life contains many other stories in which He refused to accept the prevailing view of reality. When Jesus met Mary Magdalene, who was considered an unacceptable sinner, He refused to see her the way the rest of the world did. He reached beyond consensus reality and offered acceptance, forgiveness, and love. Likewise, when Zaccheus the tax collector approached His path, Jesus didn't shun him. Instead, He expressed the wish to dine with the man— to the horror of those around Him. We likewise can choose to rise above social conditioning. We don't have to succumb to our collective cultural trance. We can choose to see things differently.

When we begin to look beyond the physical world of appearances and choose to see more than lack, we are changing the collective thought system. When enough people begin to see things differently, society's institutions and spending patterns change. Historically, fear and scarcity have led us to exploit natural resources and other people. But a wave of pioneers living in abundance will pattern the future around a new reality.

In the Sermon on the Mount, Jesus taught the abundance attitude in its purest form:

*Do not be anxious about your life, what you shall eat or what you shall drink, nor about your body, what you shall put on. Is not life more than food, and the body more than clothing? Consider the lilies of the field, how they grow: they neither toil nor spin; yet I tell you, even Solomon in all his glory was not arrayed like one of these. But if God so clothes the grass of the field, which today is alive and tomorrow is thrown into the oven, will he not much more clothe you?*

When we believe that there is already enough, we can relax and trust. We can then begin to structure our lives to reflect this belief and the expectations that flow from it. We serve the higher purpose of the whole human family by releasing our fears of lack and limitation and choosing to believe that abundance is possible. As the circle of our consciousness widens, we see the world as part of us, sharing in abundance as we are.

## Abundance and Inner Peace

*Abundance is the natural state of the Universe. We access the abundance through our open hearts.*—Arnold M. Patent, *Money and Beyond*

The abundance attitude is the conviction and deep-seated feeling that *I have enough to do what I choose now.* It is also the trust that there will be enough in the future. Abundance thinking applies to more than financial or money matters, although these are the main focus of this book. Once the feeling of abundance is understood, it can be applied to other areas of life, such as time, relationships, physical health, and happiness. Conversely, we can use the feelings of abundance we have in other areas of our lives to help us create financial prosperity.

*The only way to develop the attitude of abundance is to*

*consciously choose to accept and adopt it, moment by moment.* That probably means faking it at first, until it begins to feel natural. Whatever we focus our attention upon, that is what we will tend to experience and know increasingly in our lives. So by choosing to feel abundant, we begin to attract experiences into our lives that fit this new expectation. This doesn't mean that we manipulate situations so that they fit our expectations. On the contrary: by deliberately maintaining a stance of openness, we attract abundance to ourselves in forms that may be quite unexpected. When we let go into abundance, we assume that things are happening the way they're meant to, regardless of the appearance.

Abundance is our natural state. In their mythologies, many cultures describe an original Paradise in which the First People lived in harmony with nature, the cosmos, and one another. The Greeks and Romans believed that the world had passed through a Golden Age, in which people had known no need to plow nor to work for food. And the ancient Hebrews described a garden they called Eden, which was filled with every fruit and herb. The prophets of ancient Israel equated that original garden with the Kingdom of Heaven; later, Jesus taught that this kingdom of abundance is within each of us.

Accepting abundance as our birthright leads to inner peace and to acceptance of ourselves and of the world. *Abundance is not a destination but a process.* Happiness cannot be made to order, any more than can the feeling of being truly loved and unconditionally accepted by a mate. But we can learn to know the experience of happiness— just as we learn the art of feeling loved and fully accepted— by relaxing and enjoying the moment. Choosing to feel abundant and happy brings abundance and happiness.

Buddhism describes this way of being as neither clinging nor resisting. The Buddha taught that human suffering comes from our craving to possess things and to keep them forever, though they are impermanent. When we are in the abundance state, we flow with the river of life, in harmony with nature and with our innermost selves.

When we feel this way, we tend to have a natural and healthy desire to help and serve others. Abundance allows us to do this; as the evidences of prosperity flow into our lives, we can give money to all those we choose to support. Since we can give only what we have, allowing abundance to flow through us allows us to serve others, as well as ourselves.

Many people are already accustomed to abundance thinking when it comes to love. There is, after all, an unlimited amount of love available for giving and receiving. The more love we give, the more we have. Can you imagine a mother saying to her child, "I can't give you any more love now. I've run out of the love I have for today"? Of course, some people who have been emotionally deprived during childhood do in fact feel and act this way when they become parents; but even they would probably admit the absurdity of the scarcity attitude as it applies to love, if only they thought about it.

It is foolish and self-limiting to view love as a finite commodity in short supply. Why, then, are we in the habit of seeing time and money in this way? Perhaps because time and money can be measured more easily than can love. We can have an hour of time or a thousand dollars of money; but how can we quantify the amount of love we have? And yet, like love, money and time are capable of expanding to suit the need, if we open ourselves to that possibility through the abundance attitude. It is often said that if you need to ask a favor, you should ask a busy person, one who has mastered the art of time expansion; not an idle person, who views time as scarce.

Sometimes it helps to *visualize* abundance. Picture two children, each sitting in a sandbox on a beach. The beach, an infinite stretch of sand, extends as far as the eye can see. Each child spends a little of the sand in his box now and then, throwing it out onto the beach.

One child believes in scarcity. He is anxious about the diminishing supply in his sandbox. He hugs his pail tightly and tries to spend as little sand as possible. He is fearful of running out.

The other child believes in abundance. She freely scoops sand off the beach to put in her box and gladly shares what she has. She even expands the size of her box to accommodate the increase, and she can step out of the sandbox altogether whenever she chooses, in order to experience the infinite supply all around.

When I notice myself beginning to think in terms of scarcity, I stop and choose to change my thinking. I take some deep breaths and notice my fear and the tenseness in my body. I choose to relax and to change my mental and emotional state to one of peace and love. I say to myself, "I have enough money"—or time, or whatever I need. I use self-talk and the NLP techniques to shift into a mental state in which there is enough for me and everyone, now and always.

I use this strategy when I apply for a loan. I have been turned down in the past for a number of bank loans and mortgages. If I let myself slip into scarcity thinking, I feel anxiety and fear come up as I remember the times I have been turned down. My self-talk begins to revolve around how banks and mortgage companies dislike self-employed people. They want a copy of a W-2 and a reference from an employer, neither of which I can provide.

To shift to abundance, I consciously stop this train of thought. I remember the popular saying that banks lend money to people who don't seem to need it. I deliberately focus my attention on all the lines of credit and bank loans that I have been approved for. I remember the wonderful banker who gave me a break when I first started my business. I call to mind the conversations I have had with a friend who is in the same business I'm in. This man is worth several million dollars and earns well over $100,000 a year. He, too, has trouble getting bank loans and mortgages. He perseveres and gets what he needs, just as I do. I choose to focus on the positive and to let go of the fear. I choose to relax and trust and expect that the loan will be approved, knowing that life is a self-fulfilling prophecy.

Also, I know that sometimes, for reasons beyond my linear understanding, things don't turn out the way I expect them to. Often the way they do turn out is better for me in the long run. So I let go of attachment to the outcome of this particular loan application with this particular bank. I trust that the application will probably go through, but that if it doesn't, there are other opportunities that may prove to be better ones. I feel relaxed and at peace.

When we believe that there is enough for everyone, we begin to perceive the world differently. We become like magnets, attracting the experiences that most closely reflect the reality of abundance. This is sometimes referred to as *synchronicity,* which is defined as the appearance of meaningful coincidences or significantly related patterns of chance. In his book *Synchronicity,* Dr. David Peat calls this phenomenon "the bridge between matter and mind." We have all experienced synchronistic events. Perhaps, for example, you've received a phone call from someone you had just thought about for the first time in months or years. As we open ourselves to abundance, synchronicity increases. It becomes a natural part of our lives. Indeed, miracles can become so commonplace that we routinely figure them into our calculations!

## An Unlimited Universe

*Physical concepts are free creations of the human mind, and are not, however it may seem, uniquely determined by the external world. In our endeavor to understand reality we are somewhat like a man trying to understand the mechanism of a closed watch.*—Albert Einstein, *The Evolution of Physics*

Exposing yourself to ideas like the ones contained in this book can loosen the grip of the subconscious mind, which holds tightly to old paradigms. By breaking old thought patterns, we unleash our inner genius and open channels for the limitless, spontaneous energy of the universe to flow into our lives.

Old thought patterns can be stubborn, though, because they are reinforced by our perceptions—which are in turn conditioned by our thoughts! The sun *appears* to come up in the morning and to go down at night. We *appear* to be separate from one another. The chair I am sitting on *appears* solid. And the world *appears* to lack money and resources. But in each case, appearances are deceiving.

Astronomers realized long ago that the sun doesn't actually come up and go down. It only seems to do so from our limited perspective. It is the earth's rotation that makes the sun appear to move.

While for practical purposes we are separate from one another as human individuals, at the molecular and atomic levels we are thoroughly interconnected. Dr. Deepak Chopra says that with each breath $10^{22}$ atoms enter and leave the body. We each have within us millions of atoms that have been in the bodies of countless other human beings—and animals and trees, for that matter.

Quantum physicists have shown that "solid" matter is mostly space. Subatomic particles are separated by huge gaps, making every atom more than 99.999% empty space. Everything solid, including our bodies, is proportionately as void as intergalactic space. Moreover, subatomic particles themselves aren't solid matter in the sense that we might think; they are describable in terms of frequency and momentum. They are forms of energy.

And, while it is obvious that great numbers of people suffer from poverty, and that children in many countries are starving for want of adequate food, if we divest ourselves of certain widespread assumptions it is questionable whether there is really a lack of money or resources in the world. Wealth—particularly in our modern information-oriented society—is not created merely by the extraction and transformation of physical resources from the environment. Indeed, in most instances where wealth is being created in America today, resources and manufactured goods are only peripheral to the process. Wealth comes from new ideas and hard work at least as much as from the accumulation of "stuff." Through human inventiveness we can discover new *kinds* of resources, and we can learn to do far more with what we have. It is clear, then, that *the amount of wealth available to humanity (and to individuals) is ultimately limited only by our intelligence, ingenuity, and persistence.*

Since the world is really a continuous, dynamic flow of energy, the concepts of scarcity and lack are themselves limited, and applicable only within highly localized situations and under fixed circumstances. Outside a certain context, they make no sense. That context is the world that is generated by the collective thinking of human beings in Western civilization. By our patterns of thought, we have created a limited reality in which scarcity and lack exist. We keep these ideas in place by our shared belief in them. We have created myths and institutions that reflect and reinforce this belief. But without this massive, continual, collective affirmation, the experience of scarcity would quickly dissolve. Then, as our individual expectations and experiences began to adjust to the reality of abundance, our institutions would change to reflect our new belief.

This is one example of how our ability to see beyond prevailing paradigms grants us power. In fact, anyone who is able to rise above a widely accepted pattern of thought and to see it within a larger context is a powerful individual. Christopher Columbus had power because he knew the world wasn't flat. Living in his day, and with his knowledge, you could have bet on all the right enterprises and made a fortune.

When I visited the Mayan ruins in Mexico, I could see how desperate the inhabitants of the city of Chichen Itza had been for water. They had built a wonderful temple and covered it with masks of the rain god Chac in order to persuade him to give them more water. Think how powerful you might have been, living in that civilization, if you had been able to see beyond the consensus paradigm that the only way to get water is to construct cisterns and pray to the rain god. Imagine knowing of a secret, deep well. In those days such knowledge might have qualified you to be a ruler or a god.

In Mark Twain's *A Connecticut Yankee in King Arthur's Court*, a New Englander was mysteriously transported back in time to the age of Merlin. Once there, the man was able to gain power through his knowledge that a solar eclipse was about to occur. He pretended that he had the ability to block out the sun.

Clearly, knowledge is important. But, as Einstein and other creative geniuses have always said, imagination is more important than knowledge. That's because it takes imagination to expand the borders of our knowledge. And when we shift our perception, our imagination is set free, so that the genie part of our mind can work what appear to be miracles.

Miracles are neither scientifically impossible nor mystical; they are simply the result of the free flow of universal energy. Fritjof Capra, in his book *The Tao of Physics*, juxtaposes statements by quantum physicists and mystics. Two examples:

> *The world thus appears as a complicated tissue of events, in which connections of different kinds alternate or overlap or combine and thereby determine the texture of the whole.*—W. Heisenberg, *Physics and Philosophy*

*Things derive their being and nature by mutual dependence and are nothing in themselves.*—Nagarjuna, from *The Central Philosophy of Buddhism*

Quantum physicists and the great spiritual teachers of all traditions are in agreement that the universe is a dance of energy. Money, too, is a form of energy—the energy that we use to make things happen in our physical world. We can think of money as a manifestation of the energy of the universe.

The Latin root of the word *prosperity* means "according to hope." Prosperity comes as a result of hope, or belief, or the perception of possibility. When we think of wealth as the energy of the universe at work in the world, and when we open ourselves to that energy, then it is free to flow through us to do its work. And we ourselves are part of that endless flow, the "continual cosmic dance of energy," as Capra calls it.

*Out of mind spring innumerable things, conditioned by discrimination ... These things people accept as an external world ... What appears to be external does not exist in reality; it is indeed mind that is seen as multiplicity; the body, property, and abode—all these, I say, are nothing but mind.*—D. T. Suzuki, *Studies in the Lankavatara Sutra*

*Exercise*

## Visualization: The Abundance Waterfall

Sit in a still place, quiet your mind, and imagine yourself in the scene described below. While the term visualization implies that you will "see" the scene, you may find that your imagination is more closely connected with another sense. People who are predominantly tactile may "feel" the scene.

Auditory people are more likely to imagine what the scene sounds like. Use whatever sensory modality, or whatever combination of modalities, is right for you. You may wish to speak the words below into a tape recorder, so that you can play the tape back later and do the visualization with your eyes closed. If you do this, speak very slowly.

*Relax and take a minute to get comfortable. Breathe in deeply to the bottom of your spine for a count of four. Now hold the breath for four counts. Then let the breath out slowly, counting backwards from eight to one. Do this several times, breathing out even after all the air seems to be gone. Now just continue to be conscious of your breath going in and out through your nostrils.*

*Feel any tense muscles in your shoulders. Tense them up more, and then completely let go of the tension. Do this for any other place in your body where you feel tension. Now feel the muscles in your face and relax them, one area at a time.*

*Now imagine that you are walking through the woods. You come to the shore of a river, wide and deep. The water is clear and sparkling in the sunlight. To your left there is a large waterfall, and you hear the sound of the white water tumbling over the rocks. Relax and enjoy the beauty and peacefulness of this scene. The sun feels warm and pleasant on your body. The air is clear. Take some deep breaths and feel thankful for the beauty of nature.*

*There is an abundance of water flowing over the waterfall. There is enough water for you to take all that you want, leaving plenty for others also. Take a cupful of water. Take a few more cupfuls. Or use a bucket and take a bucketful. There is plenty. You can attach a hose and turn on the water any time you want. You don't have to save it, because there will be plenty any time you want to get more. You know you can have all the water you want now and at any time in the future. It is abundant. Notice how good it feels to know there is enough for you. You can relax and trust. You feel confident. You feel bathed in the sunlight of your abundance. Feel the joy that comes from having abundance, knowing there is plenty now and plenty more. There will always be enough for you. Feel the serenity, the peacefulness. Life is wonderful. Give thanks for your abundance. Be aware of the feeling of gratefulness and joy.*

*Pick any area of your life in which you feel abundant. You may feel abundant with respect to your family and loved ones, or in your friendships. You may feel abundant when surrounded by the beauty of nature. You may feel abundant in your ideas or specific skills, like golf; or in a hobby, like photography. Hold the vision of whatever makes you feel most abundant vividly in your mind. Be aware of exactly how your body feels when you feel abundant. Notice the relaxation that comes when you know that there is enough, that you are enough.*

*Now imagine there is an abundance of money for you. See the abundant waterfall as a waterfall of money, as much as you could ever want or use. It is an unlimited supply of money. You can take as much as you want and it has no effect on the falls. All of us can take as much as we want. There is enough for everyone. Feel yourself relax and know that THERE IS ENOUGH NOW AND THERE WILL ALWAYS BE ENOUGH.*

*Take several deep breaths and lightly press the fingers of your right hand into the palm. Feel the peace and joy of abundance. Do this again several times, feeling abundance in every cell of your body. Still taking deep breaths and clenching your right hand, see the bountiful waterfall of money flowing into your life. Hear the rumble of the cascades of water crashing over the rocks. Whenever you want to bring back this feeling, you can take a deep breath and press your fingers into your right palm, and the feeling will return.*

*Know that you can return to this feeling any time you want. You can take this wonderful feeling of abundance and apply it to any area of your life. All you have to do is relax,*

*p breath, and press together your right hand.*
*ll yourself that in a moment you will feel wide*
*awake and wonderful. You will remember the feeling of*
*abundance.*
*Now slowly begin to move your hands and feet. Remember the room you are in and how you are sitting. When you are ready, open your eyes. You are now wide awake and feeling good.*

## Exercise

## Training Our Mind: The Abundance Switch

This is an exercise to create an NLP anchor to help you consciously switch from the scarcity mind state to the abundance mind state.

Close your eyes and imagine yourself in the depths of despair. There has been a catastrophe and everything you own has been wiped out. The insurance companies have failed you. You, and many others, are homeless and hungry, with no visible way out of the crisis. Step inside the picture and let yourself taste genuine feelings of anxiety and despair.

Now, in your mind, visualize the situation I have just described as a movie being projected onto three-quarters of a giant screen; only the bottom right is free of it. At the bottom right is another scene, one filled with loving people, nature, a pleasant-looking house, piles of money—whatever makes you feel joyful, peaceful, and abundant. Use the waterfall visualization if you like. Take time to step inside a time when you felt totally secure, peaceful, and abundant. Use whatever modality you found effective in the other NLP exercises.

Now, as these feelings intensify, visualize the border of the scene at the bottom right moving up and to the left so that the entire screen is filled with abundance. Add sounds of abundance—perhaps the sound of a waterfall. Let feelings of assurance, peace, joy, and abundance fill your body. At the same time, move your thumb over the first finger of your right hand as if you were turning a knob or flipping a switch. Feel yourself consciously making the choice to feel abundant.

Practice doing this five times or more.

You can use the abundance switch in your daily life. Start with little things. If you notice yourself feeling anxious because you forgot to go to the bank and get cash, visualize the screen and do the switch. Do the switch when you are beginning to think about taking a risk on your job or making an investment. Make it a game, a dance: Do the abundance switch. In any situation, you can switch from anxiety to peace and joy.

You are in charge of your emotions. You can make the switch whenever you choose. After a while, the motion of your thumb and finger may be all you need to change fear to assurance. The experience is like walking into a dark house and turning on the lights. The power of abundance is already present; all that is needed is for you to turn on the switch.

*Exercise*

## Abundance Affirmations

Write an affirmation that pushes at the envelope of your belief system regarding abundance—one that makes you stretch, but that is not *too* uncomfortable. Once you have integrated the belief into your body, move on to another one. And for the whole of this week, practice feeling abundance. Write down your affirmation and tape it to your bathroom mirror, so that it will be one of the first things you'll see in the morning. Tape it to the dashboard of your car, so you can spend your drive to work celebrating your abundance. Do everything you can to remind yourself of the reality of abundance.

Use the NLP exercise to place the affirmation in the *believe* side of the brain. Remember to use the *believe* body position.

Start out only with what your body believes, and work up to the fullest extent of abundance that your mind can conceive. Don't affirm things that your body is clearly saying are impossible. Then, each week, push that edge out a little farther. Practice the abundance mind state!

# 8

## FREEING THE ANGEL
## FROM THE BLOCK OF MARBLE

*Positive thinking does indeed "work" when it is consistent with the individual's self image. It literally cannot "work" when it is inconsistent with the self image . . .*
——Maxwell Maltz, *Psycho-cybernetics*

*LIMITED:* I have to struggle, but somehow each month I seem to squeak by.

*EMPOWERED:* I love my work, and money flows in abundantly as a by-product.

*LESSON:* Transforming my self-paradigm can transform my experience of wealth and power.

SAY "I am Rich." How do you feel? Would you be different if you were rich? How would your family and friends treat you if you were rich? How would you feel toward others if you were rich?

Take out a blank piece of paper and magic markers and write in the center I AM RICH. Draw a circle around the words. Now do a mind map (see the exercise in chapter 3).

Are you finding issues rising up regarding your identity? Are you uncomfortable with the idea of being rich? Do you feel fearful? What judgments about rich people come up?

You may also want to mind map the phrase I AM POWERFUL. At least go back and look at your mind map on power. Blocks regarding wealth are often connected with power issues. Blocking money is an easy way to avoid having power, when power is seen as external imposition and control.

I didn't think I had any resistance to the idea of being rich.

Then I did this exercise and felt surprisingly uneasy as I tried on a wealthy identity.

For the purpose of this exercise I have used a phrase that equates identity with a quantity of money: "I am rich." It is more accurate to say, "I have wealth." However, the emotions that this exercise brings up are useful in understanding our thoughts and feelings about our identity as it relates to wealth. And it is at the core of our identity that our most basic attitudes toward wealth are grounded.

People sometimes get discouraged because their affirmations don't seem to work. Affirmations are helpful, but they cannot work when we have a self-image that contradicts them. An affirmation like "I live in abundance" will have little effect if my self-image says, "I am not smart enough to make a good living; I don't deserve to have money; I am not responsible enough to handle wealth," or "Rich people are different from me and I could never be like them." Studies of lottery winners show that if their self-image is not consistent with their new level of wealth they tend to lose their money quickly. Affirmations about having wealth work when we shift our self-image so that it is consistent with the desired result.

The purpose of this chapter is to help you reinvent your self-image. The idea isn't just to make ourselves a little better. Our goal is a radical shift in how we perceive ourselves— literally to create a new *identity* for ourselves that enables us to have wealth and power if we so choose.

## Shifting Your Self-paradigm

I am using the term *self-paradigm* instead of *self-image* in order to emphasize the all-encompassing nature of these rules of perception and action. Our self-image may rise and fall as a barometer of our day-to-day successes and failures in life. But our self-paradigm sets the boundaries within which our self-image varies; it defines the playing field in our game of life. It makes the rules and tells us what position we will play. It sets our boundaries and tells us what we can do and cannot do.

A person with a *limited* self-paradigm cannot experience wealth and inner power. If such a person acquires riches by chance, they are more a burden than a blessing, because they contradict the pre-existent self-paradigm. A limited self-paradigm encourages a person to see herself as the effect of outside forces. The external world is in charge and the person merely reacts to it.

A person with an *empowered* self-paradigm sees herself as the cause of what happens in life. The source of power is within; or, in spiritual terms, the source of power in the person's life resides in her connection to God or Higher Self. A person with the empowered self-paradigm can consciously choose to experience and enjoy abundance.

Read these sentences and feel the self-paradigm implied in each:

"I hold my breath each month, but I usually manage to squeak by."

"I hate my marriage, but I am scared to death to try and make it on my own."

"I'm too old to make a career change."

"I don't have enough education to get any kind of decent job."

"I can't imagine myself in a powerful job. It is too scary."

"I know I'm talented, but the world will never recognize my talent."

"I enjoy my work, and I always have plenty of money to do what I want."

"I get satisfaction out of doing my job well, and a good salary is a by-product."

"I get up each morning and give thanks for my happiness and my abundance in all things."

Our self-paradigm is the root from which our life grows.

No amount of feeding the leaves of a plant will nourish it; we must feed the roots.

My son Evan, two years out of college, is working as a project manager for a construction company. He tells me with amazement that the job superintendent often complains that he, twenty years Evan's senior, can't do certain things because he didn't go to college. Evan tells me he thinks this is silly because he knows that he, as a twenty-three-year-old, could certainly do those things without going to college. The job superintendent's real problem is his limiting self-paradigm.

The development of Japanese industry over the past twenty years is an excellent example of a self-paradigm shift: the Japanese transformed their image as manufacturers of low-quality products to that of makers of the highest-quality durable goods. It may be hard to remember now, but before 1960 Japanese products were generally considered second-rate, cheap, and shoddy. Barker, whose whole book is about the power of paradigms in business, calls this the most important paradigm shift of the twentieth century.

Ironically, it was from an American, W. Edwards Deming, that the Japanese first acquired the paradigm of quality control and continual improvement. Japan created a Deming Award, which became the highest industrial award in the country.

When first faced with the competition from these new quality products, American industry responded with excuses—which is one of the ways we normally respond when faced with a paradigm shift. We make excuses for our failures, without realizing that the *reason* our old strategies aren't working is that the paradigm itself has changed and requires a new set of behaviors.

Japan created a new image of itself as a manufacturer. This paradigm shift changed both its perception and its actions. The country's industry did everything from a new base.

It is possible to become conscious of our self-paradigm and to transform it. *I invite you to change the base from which you see yourself.* You are the manufacturer of your own life. Is it high-quality, or just good enough to get by? The Japanese produced a superior car, and people responded. When you reinvent yourself as a high-quality individual, people will likewise respond. I'm not talking about changing the superficial aspects of yourself; I am suggesting that it is possible for you to change *the essence of how you perceive yourself.* And this paradigm change can be the blueprint from which wealth and happiness follow.

The new Japanese self-paradigm included a commitment to a purpose—that of quality. You must have a new sense of purpose as well.

Be bold. Think big. Reinvent yourself with a clear purpose and with commitment, and expect natural abundance to flow in to support you.

Many of the ideas presented in this book may require a paradigm shift on your part in order for you merely to understand and assimilate them. If you are noticing resistance to these ideas, that is not unusual. We always resist change.

*Exercise*

## What Is My Present Self-Paradigm Regarding Money?

Write the following questions in your notebook or journal, then continue writing in response to them. Avoid one-word answers. Or, rather than writing your answers, you can tell your story to a friend or speak it into a tape recorder.

1. What is my story in relation to money? Do I have to struggle? Do I have to do work for money instead of doing what I love to do? Do I just squeak by?
2. What is my self-paradigm as it relates to money?

# Conditional Self-Esteem
## Versus Core Self-Esteem

*If I am to consider myself worthwhile, I must always achieve, win and succeed.—*Lee Jampolsky, *Healing the Addictive Mind*

*With enough sun and water to put down deep roots of self-esteem, children can withstand terrible storms. Without them, the slightest wind will seem full of danger.—*Gloria Steinem, *Revolution from Within: A Book of Self-Esteem*

There are two kinds of self-esteem. The first, which is more prevalent in our society, is *conditional self-esteem.* We *earn* this by winning approval from others and by our accomplishments. Our first successes are defined by our parents. We receive approval, acceptance, and love from them as we learn to behave as they wish, to look good, and to do well in sports or academics. *The source of conditional self-esteem is external.* The reactions of others, originally our parents, define our self-worth.

We strive to achieve conditional self-esteem by doing something well or by accumulating money, power, or accomplishments. We have to compete, achieve, and protect in order to acquire it. But in the process, we give our power away to that which we see as the source of our self-esteem. We are outer-directed, defining our worth by our external rewards. Our core is empty of worth, and we need to fill it up. Paradoxically, however, when we feel empty at the core, nothing external is capable of giving us the core feeling of self-worth for which we long.

Conditional self-esteem is like a drug that masks the symptom by filling the inner void temporarily. When it wears off, we feel the pain of withdrawal. Then it is time to go out and get some more approval, success, money, love, sex, alcohol, or pot. Perhaps then we'll feel okay again.

Fortunately, we don't have to live out our lives this way. There is another way. The second and more fundamental kind of self-worth is *core self-esteem*, which is inherent in the individual. Core self-esteem does not require continual replenishment from an external source. It springs from a constant, internal source of unconditional love and acceptance.

Core self-esteem accepts that each of us is valuable and worthy by right of birth. When we have it, we love and accept ourselves just the way we are. We acknowledge that, on the soul level, each person is perfect, whole, and complete.

Of course, each of us may have accumulated some personality characteristics that are less than perfect. But with core self-esteem we can accept those imperfections as part of the experience of being human, and we can choose to love and accept ourselves and others in spite of them. Our imperfections provide us with the starting points from which we build and transform our lives. Psychologists say that the way to change a habit is first to lovingly accept it and then to change from that place.

Michelangelo said that when he carved a statue, he carved away the excess marble to find the perfect form within. Each of us has the perfect form within us—the angel awaiting our carving away the erroneous beliefs and feelings that have imprisoned it.

When we see the core of our being as full, we are a like the constantly radiating sun. We have plenty to give and share.

Core self-esteem flows from a state of inner peace. Having inherent self-esteem doesn't mean we stop accomplishing and achieving excellence. Rather, coming from a place of inner peace, we *choose* to excel, instead of feeling pressure to excel in order to attain self-worth.

With core self-esteem we can take the risks that are necessary in order to achieve financial success. We are confident enough to break the rules. We can use our failures as valuable lessons because we do not accept failure as our identity. We say, "I made a mistake, but next time I'll do better"; never, "I am a failure." We are secure at the core, and so it is easy for us to accept change, to see and accept new opportunities, or to move into positions of financial responsibility and power.

As we acquire greater core self-esteem we can see many possibilities that we couldn't see before. We take actions that attract new opportunities to us. We present ourselves in such a way that others feel inspired to trust and support us.

Take a deep breath, close your eyes, and say: "I unconditionally love and accept myself just the way I am." How does that feel?

Some people say they feel guilty. After all, we don't wish to be—or to appear—narcissistic, egotistical, or self-centered. But core self-esteem has nothing to do with selfishness. In fact, inwardly secure people tend to be generous and compassionate; it is the insecure person, addicted to conditional self-esteem, who tends to preen or impose. When we are competing for conditional self-esteem, we tend to see life as a win-or-lose proposition. When we are inherently worthy, we can reach out and lovingly share with others and help them.

We can give only what we have. If we feel empty inside, we don't have much to give. In contrast, the person with inherent self-esteem is like an ever-full water pitcher. Perhaps the most striking example of a person with core self-esteem was Jesus, who gave from a boundless inner wellspring of love. He didn't seek to get self-esteem by fulfilling the conditions of society. Both His endless compassion and His unwavering sense of authority flowed from His innermost connection with God.

I find that the level of my core self-esteem is directly related to the degree of my awareness of the God source within. I have come to know a place of inner wisdom that is entirely different from my socially conditioned thoughts and feelings. Moreover, I can *choose* to see the world from that place.

I grew up with fairly good conditional self-esteem. I was an outstanding student and therefore received my share of external rewards. However, I did not have much core self-esteem. This showed up in my marriage, in which I displayed many of the typical signs of low self-esteem, such as dependency, submissiveness, avoidance of conflict, and the feeling of being victimized. I had to learn to give myself core self-esteem. But it took time.

For years I made the mistake of picturing my self-empowerment journey as a linear, step-by-step process of attaining a specific goal. I have learned that there is no final goal, only the process. I choose to come from my inner core of self-worth; when I notice that I have gotten off base, I choose again to return to my place of self-esteem. I coach myself, and when I get stuck I call on one of my friends with whom I have a co-coaching relationship.

I haven't met anyone with 100% core self-esteem. However, coming to understand the process of self-transformation and feeling the exquisite joy of living from the place of core self-esteem are great rewards. As I give my attention to them, the outer aspects of my life just fall into place naturally. Having tasted this way of being, I know that now I couldn't live any other way.

We can choose:

To see ourselves coming from our inner core of self-esteem.
To accept and love ourselves as we are.
To feel the joy of being inherently worthy.
To feel natural abundance flowing into our lives because we deserve it.

Psychologists have found that one way to change beliefs is to act as if they are already changed. Act from a place of having core self-esteem, and you will begin truly to have it.

When you are feeling upset, anxious, confused, or angry, ask yourself:

How would I perceive this situation from a place of core self-esteem?
How would I act from a place of core self-esteem?

Choose to act in ways that are self-enhancing and self-affirming. If you notice that something isn't working, go back and choose again.

## Freeing Our Self-Image

*We are dominated by everything with which our self is identified. We can dominate and control everything from which we dis-identify ourselves.*—Robert Assagioli, *Psychosynthesis*

In the "I am rich" exercise at the beginning of the chapter, we identified ourselves with our possessions for the purpose of a brief exercise. The Money Freedom approach, however, is "I am I, and I have wealth." Since this statement sounds a bit awkward, it can be shortened to "I have wealth." Feel the difference between "I am rich" and "I have wealth." When we say "I am," and follow it with a word that signifies a thing or a quality, we identify ourselves with that thing or quality. That becomes our identity.

We can be free to have wealth (and not be had by it) when it isn't our identity. Also, it is easier to transform our feelings of being unworthy of wealth if it is something *I have* as opposed to *who I am.* The fear of losing our money or job or house loses its power over us when we separate our possessions from our identity.

If someone asks who you are, how do you answer? A typical response would be "I am a lawyer," "I am a mother," "I am a college student," or "I am a secretary." We label ourselves, and the act of labeling limits our identity.

In truth, each of us is far more than a label. As we label ourselves, we take one aspect of ourselves and define our identity and our possibilities within its boundaries.

If my identity is limited to that of mother, it is difficult for me to add financial success to my life. If my identity is that of truck driver, then I will miss the upcoming opportunity to move into management. If I think I am my emotions, then my fear of applying for a new job will keep me from doing it.

The possibilities for living our lives depend on how we see ourselves. We are dominated by that with which we are identified. We are free to be in control when we become aware and dis-identify ourselves. We reclaim our power to be in charge of our lives when we recognize what is going on.

The following material is based on the teachings of Dr. Robert Assagioli, the founder of a school of psychology called *Psychosynthesis* (which is also the title of his book).

I have a role in life as mother, accountant, retired person, or sales clerk, and I AM NOT JUST MY ROLE. I AM MORE. The use of "I have" language frees us from labeling: I have children, I teach school, or I do accounting work.

I have possessions, and I AM NOT MY POSSESSIONS. I AM MORE. I am not my big house, my old broken-down car, or my new Porsche.

I have a body which produces physical sensations, and I AM NOT MY BODY. I AM MORE THAN MY BODY. We mistakenly identify ourselves with our body and its sensations. See the difference between saying "I am starving" and saying "My body feels hungry."

I have emotions which produce feelings, and I AM NOT MY EMOTIONS AND FEELINGS. I AM MORE. Again, we speak as though we were our emotions: "I am unhappy. I am afraid." The emotion then controls us like a puppet. A more accurate statement would be, "I feel fear." See the freedom when the "I" that I am isn't identified with the fear.

Allowing our money fears to take control is one of the major problems in achieving a state of money freedom. When we can dis-identify with the feelings and observe ourselves having these feelings, it is easier to look at the fear objectively and choose to act with assurance and clarity. When you are feeling afraid, try saying to yourself: "I am I, and I have fears about _____."

I have an intellect which produces thoughts, and I AM NOT MY INTELLECT AND MY THOUGHTS. I AM MORE. Usually we identify ourselves with our thoughts. But when we stand outside and observe our thoughts, we see that they are changeable—sometimes logical, sometimes not. We can hear our own self-talk: "I haven't got enough time to do that project right"; "I don't think I ought to take that kind of risk"; "I can't do that." We can notice our thoughts and choose to change them if we want. They don't have control over us when we are no longer identified with them.

Money freedom is attainable when we are coming from an "I" that is an aware center of will. By being aware of our spoken language and self-talk, we can stop identifying ourselves with labels, emotions, or thoughts. We can practice using language that honors our self as larger than, and independent, from the aspects of our experience.

Two identity states that often block our access to inner power and wealth are the inner critic and the frightened adult child.

One area of work that has been very helpful to me with clients is the voice dialogue technique taught by Hal Stone and Sidra Winkleman. In this work we actually talk to our inner identity states, or selves. When they are brought into our conscious awareness, these identity states lose much of their power over us.

# Dis-identifying with the Inner Critic

*My one regret is that I am not someone else.*—Woody Allen

One of our primary ways of blocking wealth is by feeling that we aren't worthy of having it. And this sense of unworthiness is constantly reinforced by one of our "selves," called the inner critic. This internal voice is never satisfied with us. It originated in the criticisms of our parents, which as children we tended to internalize and direct at ourselves. But throughout life we have added to this voice's power over us every time we've thought something negative about ourselves. The inner critic is constantly saying things like "I don't look right," "I'm not smart enough," "I don't do things the way I should," and "I'm simply not good enough."

The overpowering inner critic's debilitating effect on one's life cannot be overstated. Indeed, it is possible that some characteristics of our culture as a whole—its drivenness, its restlessness, its inability simply to enjoy nature and life without having to *make something* of them—derive from our common child-rearing practices which, being far more disciplinarian than those of so-called primitive peoples like the Native Americans or Africans, tend to instill a more active inner critic.

The inner critic beats us up; it keeps us stuck; it incapacitates us; it keeps us from being able to flow with inner power and abundance. The inner critic likes to work on other people too. Our friends, children, spouses, and fellow employees are seldom "good enough" either.

It is only by becoming aware of our inner critic that we gain the opportunity to free ourselves from it. We may never be able to fully dislodge the inner critic. To do so might not be a good idea anyway, as the faculty of conscience rests on our ability to be self-critical. But there is an important distinction to be made here: a healthy conscience assesses the moral quality of our *actions*; the overblown inner critic, on the other hand, constantly picks away at our *identity* and self-worth. We can learn to distinguish between the former and the latter, and to largely ignore the internal voice of self-doubt. One way to do this is to mimic it and laugh at it. Or we can thank it for sharing and then shrug off its criticism.

The inner critic sounds like this:

"How could you be so stupid?"

"You don't deserve to have money. You wouldn't know how to handle it even if you had it."

"Don't apply for that new position. Even if you got it, you'd just blow it and get fired."

"Why haven't you got a better job? You should be able to do something more worthwhile with your life."

"When are you ever going to learn?"

"Just shut up and no one will find out how little you know."

One client with an active inner critic told me that all she saw in the mirror was wrinkles and her stomach sticking out.

Another, George, had a string of outstanding accomplishments. He had held a high post in government, he had created his own computer software program that sold for $10,000 a copy, and he had written several books. Yet he was very dissatisfied with himself. His inner critic kept reminding him that none of his books had been a best-seller and that he didn't get $15,000 per speaking engagement like George Will. He told me that he didn't measure up to the people he compared himself with. The critic can always find someone who is more successful than ourselves, smarter than we are, in better shape, or more spiritual.

Detaching ourselves from our inner critic is a highly effective step toward internal power and deep-seated peace. Begin to listen to your self-talk. Be aware of the inner critic.

It is always dissatisfied, so it is easy to recognize. Then begin deliberately to ignore it.

Our critics have different personalities. I don't have the constantly harping critic that some people seem to put up with. Instead, I have a somber judge in black robes who monotonously pronounces the verdict: "Not good enough." It is useful to listen for evidence of other people's inner critics, as it helps us to recognize and dis-identify with our own.

You can also use the NLP *changing intensity* exercise on the inner critic. Turn down the voice so it is hardly audible. Add static. Add another voice, that of an angel singing "You are wonderful"—as if the radio were bringing in two stations at once. If your critic has a face, make it faint. Let a fog roll in between you and the face. Feel a wave of loving energy washing over you and the critic. You might see the critic feeling foiled by this wave of loving energy. Be playful and see what works best for you personally. Don't resist the critic, because that gives it power. Rather, play games with it. Remember: giving it love disarms it.

## Creating Your Customized Money-Master Personality

Ask yourself: What identity state are you in when you deal with money issues? Many people are surprised to realize that, when the subject is money, their confident, competent adult self gives way to a more childish self with less appropriate emotional perceptions and responses.

I have clients who are brilliant, talented, capable people who cannot make a decent living. These people habitually have an identity state I call the *financial adult child* in charge of money matters. The person may operate effectively in other areas of life, but somehow he or she has gotten stuck in a child's view of the world when it comes to money. The problem is that the child acts entirely on the basis of emotion; and, while emotions are an essential part of life, they often steer us wrong unless balanced by more rational perceptions and judgments.

For example: Susan is intelligent and highly motivated, and she works hard. She has written a book, although she hasn't been able to find a publisher for it. It seemed that nothing she did made money. She had once worked as a sales trainer; but she kept coming up with ideas to do the training differently, and her boss was unreceptive to her suggestions. At another point, she had had her own business working in public relations for companies seeking contracts with the government. When I began to work with her, she was trying to decide what to do with her life. She had just started another business, consulting and coaching people to overcome their anxieties, fears, and blocks to success.

While I was working with Susan regarding her financial issues, her frightened adult child peered out and confessed to me that she "didn't know how the world worked." She said that no one had ever taught her. Then she admitted that deep down she had always felt unsafe in the world. To really understand and effectively operate in the financial sphere seemed beyond her grasp.

I realized that I was working with a person who, in finances, was functioning as an adult child. Naturally, seeing from a child's perspective, she couldn't understand how the world worked. The adult world *is* hard to figure out, especially for a young child growing up with an alcoholic parent; and this had been the story of Susan's childhood.

When she understood the source of her financial fears, she stopped berating herself for her failures. I helped her develop a "powerful money expert" adult identity inside herself, and I guided her to act from that personality. She began to bring this part of herself into play in her work, and her business started to grow by leaps and bounds. Her mode of dress changed, and so did the way she expressed herself. She began to project an aura of personal power that

brought in new clients easily. The "money master" personality transformed more than just her financial situation. By
mastering money, Susan accessed her inner sense of power.

A highly successful psychotherapist who was making a
good living told me that she hated to deal with money and
did a poor job of it. I got the sense that she felt that dealing
with money was an "inferior" use of her time. On several
occasions she had hired someone to take care of her financial affairs, but she had had bad luck with these people.

First, we worked out a scheme whereby she created an
*internal* money manager who was an "admirable" person.
For a model, we picked Ben Cohen of Ben & Jerry's Ice
Cream, because he is financially successful and committed
to empowering employees and supporting social causes.
Her money-manager self was then able to hire a competent
and trusted outside consultant to handle her finances, and
she was able to cooperate with the consultant.

The money-mastering personality can have any configu-
ration you choose it to have in order to fit your particular
circumstances. It is essential, however, that it not be based
on the fearful child. When we are in the fearful child identity, we look out and see impossible situations. But once we
consciously shift our identity state to that of money master,
the situation looks completely different. When Einstein said
that the problem cannot be solved at the same level at
which it was created, he was saying that we need to shift to
a new perspective in order to find the solution.

Shifting identities from that of fearful child to that of
money master is like climbing from a dense forest up a
mountainside. Our vision constantly expands. The essential characteristic of the money master is that she or he is a
confident, trusting adult who can disengage from a fearful
or childish perspective and make conscious choices. It is an
identity state based on inner power, with our deepest self as
the source of that power. The money master sees the money
world as a mirror and knows that to change his experience

)rld he must change his thoughts. The money mas-
--. .- .-. charge.

Each of us already has at least the germ of a powerful inner person who can take charge. Use the process described below to get to know that part of yourself and to begin to mold it into a competent, capable financial master who fits your particular needs. When you have trained yourself to recognize when your fearful child identity is taking control, and when you have learned to dis-identify from it, then you can consciously shift to the money-master identity.

We are adding a new aspect to our self-paradigm.

The financial master:

is a capable adult;
has inner power;
operates from conscious choice;
can see from the perspective of outside observer;
has core self-esteem;
has trust in self and in the world; and
has a context of love and abundance.

*Exercise*

## Being the Money Master

To access your customized internal money master, first set aside some quiet time. You may want to take a quiet walk in nature or to meditate. Then *ask* to meet the part of yourself that is describable by the phrases above. You can also ask to contact your inner money master in a dream. Do a mind map on your money master. Your awareness of the money master will develop and expand over time. Begin with the intention, and let the experience unfold.

Once you have made contact, the next step involves role playing. You must get to know what it feels like to *be* the money master. This identity state has a high energy level.

Simply act the part. In the beginning you will feel foolish, as though you are faking it, but the money-master identity will become real as you flesh it out. You may want to record yourself on tape so you can listen to this new self. You may also want to use a video camera. Practice the money-master identity until you move into it naturally.

One way to orchestrate your role playing is to use a standard Gestalt technique. Arrange two chairs facing each other. When you are sitting in one chair, you are your "normal" self; in the other, you are the money master. Ask a question while sitting in the "normal" chair, and then change chairs and answer from the identity state of money master.

Another technique involves writing. Initiate a dialogue on paper with your dominant hand. Allow the money master to reply using the nondominant hand. Both these exercises can move from a question-and-answer format into free discussion.

Feel free to customize your role-playing experiments. In the case of one client, who was having a problem getting in touch with his feeling of inner power, I set up mock business situations in which he performed as a capable and powerful salesperson. On other occasions I've interviewed clients as though we were five years in the future and they—in their respective money-master identities—were explaining how they had become so successful. In one instance I played the role of well-known TV talk-show hosts interviewing my client's money master. The experience was so exhilarating that we then reversed roles so I could play, too. This approach can be lots of fun.

## Mirror Exercise

The secret to having abundance is unconditionally loving and supporting all aspects of ourselves and others. When we judge, we block the energy flow. When we judge ourselves not worthy, obviously we block ourselves from having abundance. And when we judge others as bad because they have wealth, we also block ourselves from receiving. The universe is abundant, but we block the flow.

Look in the mirror and tell yourself: "I unconditionally love and accept you just the way you are." Notice if parts of your body pop out that are unacceptable. Choose to love them. When we judge and reject a part of ourselves, we are blocking the flow of abundance energy.

Remind yourself:

I am an extension of God's perfect love energy, and I allow myself to be fulfilled in all aspects of my life.
I accept all love and support.
I accept all abundance for myself and others.

## Affirmations

These are some suggested affirmations. Try writing some of your own. Repeat them while looking in a mirror.

I am good enough to have wealth.
I deserve to have wealth.
I choose to have wealth.
I have wealth.
I have more and more wealth each day.
I unconditionally love and accept myself just the way I am.
I recognize and laugh at my critic.
I am perfect, whole, and complete just the way I am.
I love and accept myself and others.

# 9

# SEEING A SAFE AND SUPPORTIVE WORLD

*Two men looked out through prison bars. One saw mud,*
*the other saw stars.* —Anon.
*Change your thoughts and you change your world.*
—Norman Vincent Peale

*LIMITED:* I feel that the world is not a safe place.

*EMPOWERED:* I feel safe and supported in the world,
and I know that I determine how I see the world.

*LESSON:* I can transform my mental models of the world.

AS WE saw in chapter 4, our paradigms constitute unquestioned sets of assumptions that control how we experience reality—what we perceive and how we respond. In his seminal book on learning organizations, *The Fifth Discipline: The Art and Practice of the Learning Organization,* and in his work with major corporations, management consultant Peter Senge uses the term *mental model* in place of the word *paradigm;* he explains how our mental models of the world can sabotage our experience of wealth and inner power.

As an example, Senge describes the recent evolution of the American automobile industry. Only three decades ago, the Big Three automakers "knew" that the American public bought cars on the basis of styling, not for their quality or dependability. This was an accurate assumption—until the Germans and Japanese began to educate American consumers to appreciate the benefits of quality and dependability in cars. Management consultant Ian Mitroff, in his book *Break-Away Thinking,* lists the assumptions that controlled the actions of General Motors:

- GM is in the business of making money, not cars.
- Cars are primarily status symbols.
- Styling is therefore more important than quality.
- The American car market is isolated from the rest of the world.
- Workers do not have an important impact on productivity or product quality.
- No one connected with the system has need for more than a fragmentary, compartmentalized understanding of the business.

Gradually, of course, the Germans and the Japanese increased their share of the American car market, from 0% in the mid-1950s to 38% by 1986. The "world"—insofar as the American car buyer was concerned—had changed, but for years the American automobile manufacturers held onto their old, largely unconscious assumptions. These beliefs led them to take transparently ineffective actions in their attempts to regain their share of the car market.

As individuals, we sabotage ourselves in similar ways. Our parents taught us their mental models of the world, and we naturally absorbed and accepted many of these, perhaps in spite of our occasional attempts to rebel against them. In addition, we may have acquired self-defeating money myths, such as those we examined in Chapter 3, from other sources. These assumptions and myths are like self-fulfilling prophecies: because they shape the way we perceive the world, it is virtually impossible for us to receive information that contradicts them. We *interpret* what we see in terms of our mental model, and then we *take our interpretation as proof of the model's correctness.* The following story illustrates what I'm talking about.

Sarah was brought up in a lower-middle-class family. Her father was a government accountant who hated his job. There were six children in the family, and her mother and father often worried about lack of money. They soberly advised the children to get good educations in solid fields so that they would be financially secure later in life. When Sarah was nearing high-school graduation she declared her desire to study psychology. Her parents were furious. They told her that this was a "soft" subject that would offer her no future. Four years later, she received a degree in accounting.

Her first job was as a bookkeeper. She made a good salary but found that she dreaded going to work each day. Gradually, in her spare time she involved herself in programs to end hunger in the world. This work was far more fulfilling than her job, so she quit bookkeeping and began raising funds for worthy projects. She became widely respected in her new career. However, in administrating each project she made certain that everyone working for her got paid first, so that she always wound up with barely enough to pay the rent. When she did get a little ahead financially, she would plow her money into yet another worthy project.

When Sarah came to see me she was in debt and couldn't see her way out. I asked her to envision herself several years in the future doing the work she loves *and* having financial security. She tried; then suddenly she burst into tears. "I can't do it," she exclaimed. The child in her still believed that the world would financially support only those people who engaged in what her parents described as "hard" disciplines, like accounting, engineering, and medicine. She knew intellectually that that was ridiculous, but her emotional inner child was still operating on the basis of the old mental model. She was sabotaging herself so that her experience of the world would continue to conform to her unconscious expectations.

Sarah is now in the process of transforming her basic assumptions. She has created a new vision for herself: she knows now that she can do the work that she loves *and* be financially secure. Every day she focuses on the result that she chooses to produce. Miracles have begun to happen.

Recently, against formidable odds, she was awarded a sizable foundation grant. She enjoys her work as much as ever and is even more effective in helping the causes she has chosen to champion. Moreover, for the first time in her life there is the potential for real abundance.

It is important to realize that our mental models can command our emotions. Self-sabotaging mental models are designed to produce failure; when they do, our response may be frustration or anger—which we direct not toward the model, but toward ourselves or others. Often, then, we resolve simply to try harder. This brings on more failure, and therefore more "proof" that the world is the way our mental model says it is. Only by questioning our assumptions and transforming our mental models can we break out of the vicious circle and create a new pattern of perception and action that serves our conscious purpose.

## Tuning In a New Mental Model

Our mental model of the world directly affects our experience with money. But how do we shift from a self-sabotaging model to one that more accurately reflects our conscious choices and goals? First, we must convince ourselves that *we have a choice.*

I remember when I first got cable television. There were so many channels! I often spent more time checking what was on all these new channels than I spent watching any one program. Each channel was like a different reality—an all-news reality, an all-comedy reality, a reality of nothing but weather—and all it took to change realities was the pressing of a button.

Changing mental models is not quite as easy as pressing a button, but the following cable-television analogy does serve to illustrate the fact that there are many "realities" available to us. Most of us spend our entire lives living out a single mental model. That's like watching the same channel day in and day out. Simply by becoming aware that other mental models—and therefore other realities—are available, we make it easier for ourselves to make a change.

The channels that most of us are familiar with play only reruns of tragic soap operas:

Channel 28. *The World Is Scary.* All the characters on this channel are afraid to take risks. They know that if they ever had much money it would probably be stolen. They believe that their lives are entirely controlled by external circumstances. As long as they stay small and powerless, they will be safe. They are convinced that it is good to have a "safe" job, like being a secretary or a clerk in a department store, where there isn't much risk of doing something wrong.

Channel 11. *The World Does Me In.* This channel specializes in stories about people who are victims of the world. Nothing they do seems to work. Most of the stories are about poverty and helplessness. Many of the characters are welfare recipients.

Channel 13. *It's a Dog-Eat-Dog World.* Every program on this channel is about competition and survival. Some of the characters manage to pile up a certain amount of money, but they tend to have heart attacks and die at an early age. No one trusts anyone else. There are no heroes, only survivors.

But it is important to be aware that we are capable of tuning in other channels as well:

Channel 2. *The World Is a Wonderful Place of Challenges.* Program after program features people who have made the most of their abilities and opportunities, overcoming seemingly insurmountable obstacles. This channel specializes in success stories in which there are no losers, only winners—people discovering their own inner power and creativity.

Channel 3. *The World Is a Place of Natural Abundance.* The characters portrayed are all in the process of discovering that they already have everything they need; and that as they give of themselves, ask, and trust, the Universe gives to them in return. The forms this abundance takes are sometimes surprising, but always perfect.

There are many variations, but the point is clear and simple: Some channel-realities have an anxious or fearful quality, while others are pervaded by ease, trust, and abundance. And we tune in our reality according to the mental model we hold.

*The world we experience reflects our state of mind and emotions.* When some people realize this profound truth, and see that their world is full of pain and failure, they simply blame themselves for having destructive thoughts and feelings. This is not the point. The point is that if we are willing to see and accept the truth, we can set ourselves free. We can use the world as a feedback system that allows us constantly to correct our course and adjust our mental models until we are getting in life what it is that we truly desire.

When I was first divorced, the world felt scary. This feeling was reflected in my having a negative cash flow of $20,000 the first year. My financial situation changed as I began to alter my self-paradigm and my mental model of the world. I now experience the world as a loving, supportive place. When things aren't working for me, I look inside to see what kinds of thoughts or feelings are blocking me. I identify the old fearful thoughts still emanating from my subconscious mind, and then I begin the process of transforming my mental models and my emotional state.

## The Don Quixote Game

In the play *Man of La Mancha,* Don Quixote sets up a failure-bound scenario for himself by dreaming the "impossible dream" and tilting at windmills. In real life we often set up scenarios that are just as self-defeating. This generally happens when our subconscious mind believes that the world "out there" does not support us.

People set up subtle Don Quixote games when they don't tell themselves the truth about who they are and what the real situation is. Their game is doomed to fail no matter how wonderful their vision. But the player gets to continue the quest by refusing to take responsibility for his or her part in the endeavor's failure.

For example, Suzanne has created the self-image of a brilliant person who can save the world with a special training program that she has developed. However, she can't begin her program on a small scale and build it gradually, because her Don Quixote self-image requires that it be done on a grand scale. So she spends her time applying for large grants or being angry at the world because it doesn't support her. She rejects the advice that she could start small and prove herself and her teaching method. She has created an impossible dream that she hasn't the experience or capability to fulfill.

In the beginning of an enterprise, one naturally expects a certain amount of failure or rejection. It is only when one dismisses the message of these failures and refuses to adjust course that a Don Quixote pattern sets in.

This is not to say one should give up if success isn't immediate. As in sailing, one begins by setting a course; but if the wind isn't just right, the experienced sailor tacks back and forth to make general progress in the desired direction. A good sailor will pay close attention to the wind, retrimming the sails and adjusting course frequently. The same principle holds in space flight: NASA doesn't simply send vehicles straight up into space. On-board computers must constantly make minute adjustments in order for the rocket to achieve orbit. Like sailboats or rockets, we use the world as a feedback system in order to keep ourselves moving in the direction of our goals.

Chuck made several million dollars quickly through a real estate development company that pulled some slightly gray deals. Then, according to Chuck, his partner turned on him and he lost everything. A few years later he developed another scheme that involved selling aircraft parts to foreign governments; his new partner colluded with a military official to loot the company's funds. This pattern of betrayal goes back to Chuck's childhood, when his father abandoned the family after revealing that he had been keeping a mistress. It was then that Chuck first felt betrayed. Much later in life, he realized that he was continually setting himself up to reexperience his childhood emotional trauma. He worked at forgiving his father, and the pattern of his life changed. When I last heard from him, he had successfully wheeled and dealed his way into another fortune, but his attitude was no longer one of cheating or being cheated by anyone.

The payoff for believing that the world "did it to me" is that we don't have to change or take responsibility. It isn't our fault. The disadvantage is that we give our power away to the world "out there" and we are at its mercy.

When we adopt the *inner power* approach, instead of blaming the world we take responsibility and choose to change our relationship to the world. We can step into the "outside observer" role and coach ourselves. We can ask ourselves, "What is this experience reflecting about me? What can I learn from this so I don't have to repeat the lesson? What can I do to get the results that I choose?"

## Reclaiming our Power from the World

*People are always blaming circumstances for what they are. I don't believe in circumstances. The people who get ahead in this world are the people who get up and look for the circumstances they want, and if they can't find them, make them.*—George Bernard Shaw

*I am not a victim of the world I see.*—A Course in Miracles

*When you hold resentment toward another, you are
bound to that person or condition by an emotional link
that is stronger than steel.*—Catherine Ponder

Dr. Deepak Chopra tells the following fable from his native India. There was a poor villager who possessed two
things he loved greatly—his sixteen-year-old son and a
pony. One day his pony vanished, and the villager was distraught. He stayed depressed until three days later, when
the pony returned, followed by a handsome black Arabian
stallion. The man was now overjoyed.

His son asked if he could ride the wild stallion. The father, who could not deny his son anything, bridled up the
horse. An hour later the father learned that his son had
fallen from the horse and shattered his leg in two places.
When he saw his injured son, the villager's happiness
turned to deep sorrow.

He was sitting in front of his hut crying, when soldiers
came to the house. War was imminent, and they were dragging off all the eligible boys to serve in the army. When they
saw that this man's son was maimed, they left him behind.
The father's sorrow now turned to great joy, and he gave
thanks for the accident that he had just been so depressed
over.

This fable has no ending. The man sees his life as controlled by the external world—his son and the pony—and
his happiness depends entirely upon what happens to
them.

When we see the external world as being in charge of our
lives, we have no inner power. The alternative way of seeing
the world is as a learning ground. We are in charge of our
lives, and our experiences help us to grow and learn. It becomes a challenge to discern the lesson. The world mirrors
our beliefs, reminding us that there may still be limiting
patterns hidden in our subconscious.

Lawrence E. Harrison, in his book *Who Prospers?* cites his

cross-cultural survey indicating that cultural values, or shared perceptions of the world, have a profound effect on economic success. He concludes that the successful culture—like the successful individual—sees life as "something I will do"; for the unsuccessful, life is "something that happens to me."

We are stuck as long as we feel that a person, place, or thing "did it to us."

We are stuck as long as we are angry at "them."

We are stuck when we see ourselves as victims.

We are stuck when we see ourselves occupying the high moral ground, always "right," while *they* are always "wrong."

As long as we think this way, *they* are in a position of power over us. We have given away our power and have become the effect of another person's actions or of some circumstance.

The other day I was besieged by a homeless person screaming at me about how the world had done her in. She obviously had some emotional problems. I got to thinking about it and realized that she was just exaggerating what many ordinary, "sane" people say to themselves all the time. *Such people focus their attention on what has been done to them.* And this makes them feel powerless. They try to take back some power by emphasizing that they are "right" and the other is "wrong," but even if they are somewhat successful in this it still does not give them the freedom to create as they choose. It simply sets up an unrealistic, adversarial attitude that often blocks happiness and financial abundance. *The way back to inner power is to take responsibility for the situation and to take the action necessary to produce the result you want.*

It is natural for us to feel anger in some situations. However, we can communicate clearly about how we feel and *express* our feelings, so that we clear up a situation right away rather than repressing the anger and holding onto it. The next step is to release any left-over blocks about the situation and choose to see it differently.

When we have unforgiven enemies—parents, employers, former spouses, or business partners—it is hard to feel fully safe in the world. If we believe that *they* did it to us, we will believe others can do it to us also. The world is therefore a dangerous place. If we fear someone doing us harm, we will tend to attract someone to fulfill our expectations. Beware of what you expect. On the underlying energy level, you actually bring it into your life.

The first step to being able to experience a safe and supportive world is to reframe the way we look at our past negative experiences. Only forgiveness and reframing the experience sets us free. This is the path to inner peace.

Forgive the world. Forgive yourself for anything and everything that you may seem to have done wrong, and for everything you think you should have done. Go beyond the world of appearances and realize that there has been a higher purpose in all the experiences you have ever had. They have been lessons in growth that, on some level, you chose to learn something from. Let go of all the pent-up feelings, and allow love to flow in to replace resentment. Now you are free to experience peace, freedom, and opportunity.

The Lord's Prayer gives us this advice: *Forgive us our trespasses, as we forgive those who trespass against us.*

When I got divorced, I began to make friends with other divorced people, many of them newly divorced. I noticed that they seemed to fit predominantly into two categories. There were those who were still angry at their former spouses and stayed imprisoned in that relationship of resentment. One had a heart attack; another became an alcoholic; and another had constant bouts of colitis. The other group had let go of the resentment, had forgiven the past, and had made a decision to move on with their lives. They were in various stages of readjustment and growth. When I checked back on all these people five years later, the first group were mostly in the same place. The second group had grown emotionally and were doing quite well.

When I met Laura, she was chronically in debt and living in a rented room in a basement. She told me stories of being consumed by anger and resentment and feeling racked with stomach pain. The doctors could find nothing wrong. She was angry at her father for dying when she was three years old; at her mother for not loving her and for treating her badly; at the world for taking her first husband in the war after only three years of marriage; and, as she found out when she began to do personal-growth work, she was angry at God for everything. She underwent intensive counseling for a few years and joined a Unity church and a Course in Miracles group. She began to forgive the world for taking her first husband. She got in touch with the fear her mother had felt as a stranger in a new country bringing up four children with little money.

As she let go of the anger, Laura began to look and act different. The pain in her stomach subsided. She had been working as a clerk typist. She went back to school and became a successful psychotherapist, and she now owns a lovely home and has no financial worries. Living from a place of inner power and peace, she is positively affecting others by teaching them the power of forgiveness that she has learned. The ministers in her church now refer troubled people to Laura, and they say she helps them as no one else can.

Roger had been upset for years. He had gone to Brazil to shoot a film on saving the rain forest, expecting environmental groups to support him financially. He had borrowed money from relatives, and he could borrow no more. He needed only $20,000 more to finish the film, but no one would give it to him. Roger stopped filming and spent the next two years feeling demoralized. His debt became, in his words, a physical burden weighing him down. He felt let down by the world, especially by his friends in the environmental movement. His creativity, productivity, and finances were suffering.

When I worked with him, we looked for a way to shift his perception of the experience and to help him reclaim his inner power. As he was recalling the experience, I asked him for other possible interpretations. Suddenly he became excited. "I've got it!" he exclaimed. "It was too dangerous for me to complete the film, and on some level I stopped myself by not being able to get the money." He remembered how one person whom he had filmed had disappeared. Another family had asked him to remove them from the film for fear of reprisals from the logging companies. He had ignored these incidents. But now he remembered how, a year later, a magazine exposé had created havoc and ruined some of the good work that was being done to save the forest.

When I saw Roger two weeks later, he was full of enthusiasm for the new freedom he felt. A new project was in the works, and he was receiving support for it already. It was as though he had been released from a prison. His mood was ecstatic, and he could hardly contain his enthusiasm as he recounted the events of the past two weeks.

The way to reclaim our power is to shift our perception and to forgive ourselves and all others in the situation. When we can truly shift our perception, as Roger did, forgiveness is automatic; we realize that the experience happened for a higher good and that there is really no one who needs to be forgiven. We reclaim our power once we are again in charge of our world.

## Affirmations

I forgive myself and everyone else for everything that has happened to me.

I release all resentment and judgment against others.

I look beyond the appearances and trust that there was a

higher purpose for these experiences.
I choose to forgive and to experience inner peace.

If you have a specific issue that you are angry about, create an affirmation for it. For example: "I forgive my boss and myself for the misunderstanding that happened. I choose to see it differently."

## Life as a Learning Experience

*Every adversity has the seed of an equivalent or greater benefit.*—W. Clement Stone

When we see life as a learning experience, there is no such thing as failure. There is only the opportunity to grow.

Martha graduated from a good college. She got a job as a research analyst with the federal government, which filled her with excitement and high expectations. She didn't get along with her boss, though, and was let go during a period of layoffs. Then she got a job as a researcher for *National Geographic*, but again she had disagreements with her boss. Years later she would tell me it was all her bosses' fault; she was sure that she was right and they were wrong.

At the age of twenty-eight, Marsha gave up hopes for a challenging position and took a job as a store clerk so that she wouldn't be fired again. She spent the next twenty years living at the edge of poverty, demoralized and feeling cheated by life. How different her life could have been if only she had examined her pattern of not getting along with her bosses and used her self-examination as a basis for learning and growth.

Tom Watson was also fired from his job. He too could have seen himself as a failure. But instead of focusing on what "they" had done to him, he put his energy into a new project and started the business that became IBM.

If Abraham Lincoln had allowed setbacks to stop him, he

would never have become our President. His list of apparent "failures" was daunting:

Failed in business at age twenty-one.
Defeated in a legislative race at age twenty-two.
Failed again in business at age twenty-four.
Suffered the death of his sweetheart at age twenty-six.
Had a nervous breakdown at age twenty-seven.
Lost a congressional race at age thirty-four.
Lost a congressional race at age thirty-six.
Failed in an effort to become Vice President at age forty-seven.
Lost a senatorial race at age forty-nine.

Then, at age fifty-two, Lincoln was elected President of the United States.

According to legend, Thomas Edison tried unsuccessfully 9,999 times to invent the light bulb; after still another dud, someone asked him if he was discouraged. He replied, "I didn't fail. I just discovered another way not to invent the light bulb."

How we frame our experience determines what it means to us. It is up to us to frame our experience with the world in such a way that we empower ourselves.

I use the world as a mirror. It feeds back to me what I am doing right and what I am doing wrong. It tells me what is hidden in my subconscious mind. But I have learned not to use the world's feedback as a basis for criticizing myself or others. Rather, I find I can observe compassionately and choose to learn whatever lesson is being offered.

When we find basic patterns recurring in our lives, though they may be clothed with different faces and circumstances, we can be sure that we are acting out unresolved inner conflicts. We can begin to get at the root of these conflicts by taking note of the patterns and saying to the world, "Mirror, mirror on the wall, what are you telling me today?"

In the later part of my marriage I felt like a victim. After I got divorced, I began to feel like a victim of my boss at work, and a victim of the system that would not allow me to make enough money to sustain myself. Fortunately, it was at that time that I began the work of personal growth, assessing and changing my concepts of myself and the world. Otherwise I might still be a brave, struggling person, trying hard but without much success.

I began using money as a feedback mechanism to confirm that I was on the right path: each time I made a breakthrough in my personal growth, I made a large sum of money.

I took note of negative feedback, too. When I was denying my feelings about the breakup of a relationship, I proceeded to have a car accident. Since this was a repeat of a previous incident, it got my attention: here was a pattern developing. I then began to do some serious work around admitting my feelings and accepting the part of me that felt wounded.

Though I try to learn from each of life's experiences, I do make the request to Higher Power that my lessons be pleasant. I don't subscribe to the "No pain, no gain" school of thought.

I find that when I see the world as a lesson there are no "bad" experiences. There are only puzzles to figure out. The metaphysical law is that if we don't learn from a lesson the first time, we get it again. So I look carefully to figure out what is really going on. Often another person's perspective can be helpful.

Mastery of life comes when we see our life as a learning experience and we use our experiences to correct our course.

## Trusting the World

*How deceived was I
to think that what I feared
was in the world,
instead of in my mind.*

—A Course in Miracles

*According to your faith so be it unto you.*—Matthew
9:29

There is an old story about a man who drove into a small
town out West and stopped and asked a farmer, "What is
this place like?" In reply, the farmer asked him, "What was
the last place you lived in like?" When the man answered
that it was a town of fighting and of stingy, selfish people,
the farmer responded that this was the same kind of place.
Later that afternoon another man came into town and
asked the farmer the same question. Again the farmer
asked, "What is the place like where you come from?" This
man answered that he came from a wonderful town where
the people were generous and all helped each other, especially if someone was in trouble. "Well," said the farmer, "this
is the same kind of place."

We create our own experience of the world. It is therefore
up to us to replace mistrust of the world with trust. Each
time feelings of fear or of being "alone against the world"
come up, we can choose to feel loved, safe, and supported.

Children of alcoholics and of dysfunctional families often have great difficulty trusting the world. Their early envi-
ronments were filled with confusing and conflicting
messages. For some, the consequent distrust results in financial problems; for others it may lead to addictions or
relationship problems.

A client came to me who had been unsuccessfully looking for a job for nine months. She was intelligent and quali-

fied. After working with her for a short time, I could see that she was afraid that the world would hurt her. Her bosses in her last two jobs had treated her badly. On further exploration, I learned that the treatment she received from both bosses was similar to the way she had been treated by her abusive father. Now her unconscious mind was keeping her "safe" by causing her to fail at finding another job—because if she did, she might be controlled and mistreated yet again. Consciously, she was working hard at job hunting, changing her resumé, and taking qualifying courses; but all the while, her subconscious was blocking her. When she finally recognized the source of her problem, she began slowly to work her way out. Now she has a highly successful business and is a sought-after public speaker.

We can practice projecting trust and support, and thereby we will begin to draw supporting experiences into our lives. Just as a skyscraper is built one story at a time, so we begin one step at a time. With friends, try letting go into total trust. Remember: You will get what you expect. If you say to yourself, "I will try what she says, but I know it isn't true," you will be right. But if you let go to the process—and *believe* that you can trust the world—you will be right.

Start focusing on the ways that you can and do trust the world and feel supported. What you focus on expands. Which friends make you feel supported? What kinds of activities make you feel good about yourself? Emphasize these in your life.

One of the powerful effects of the various twelve-step programs, as well as church gatherings and other support groups, is that they create a safe world for people. In the atmosphere of support, people begin to see themselves differently and experience the world differently. Is there a support group that suits your needs? Often the same effect can be derived from a co-supporting relationship with a friend or family member.

## Affirmations

You can use the gradual approach I have explained earlier as a way of leading up to these more powerful affirmations, if that seems appropriate. For example, begin with saying "I can feel . . . " and work your way up to "I am . . . "

I am safe in the world.
I trust the world.

One of my favorite series of affirmations about the world is:

I love and support me.
I love and support others and the world.
The world loves and supports me.

The world reflects our feelings about ourselves. When we don't trust ourselves, we project that distrust outward by not trusting the world. So to be able to trust the world, we begin by trusting ourselves. The second affirmation above speaks of giving of love and support to others because, on a metaphysical basis, we get what we give. So if we want something, we must first be willing to give it to others.

You can alter these affirmations to deal with specific circumstances. For example:

I love and support me.
I love and support publishers.
The world of publishers loves and supports me.

## Trusting a Higher Power

One of the best ways to experience deep trust in the world is to believe in a Higher Power. It doesn't matter how this is conceptualized—as a personal God, the God energy within each of us, nature, universal mind, or the Tao. For me, Higher Power is the basis of my deep trust and the basis of my purpose in life. I believe that my life has a deeper or higher purpose than just this physical existence on earth.

There is a story in the Old Testament, II Kings 4:1-7, about a widow who had been left destitute by her husband's death. According to Talmudic law her creditors could take her sons to satisfy her debt. She cried out to the prophet Elisha, "What can I do?" He asked her what she had in the house. She replied, "I have only one pot of oil." He was asking her about her consciousness. Her lack of faith in the Universe was reflected in her statement that she had *only* one pot of oil. Elisha told her to go to her neighbors and borrow additional pots. He was telling her to expand her trust. She poured the oil from her pot into the new vessels, and it poured freely until all the vessels were filled. As she expanded her trust, the external circumstances fulfilled that trust.

I believe that is what Jesus was teaching when He said, *"Seek first his kingdom and his righteousness, and all these things shall be yours as well."* (Matthew 6:33) I believe that His message is that we must do the inner work of trust first; the external, physical confirmation or effects will show up later.

Other Biblical passages illustrate the benefits of trust in a Higher Power. Psalms 23:1 says, *The Lord is my shepherd, I shall not want.* Jesus' Sermon on the Mount, quoted in chapter 7 (on abundance), is probably the greatest statement ever made on trust and the way to receive abundance.

When we tune in to the underlying dimension of unlimited abundance, we can begin to manifest it in our lives. The process begins with our faith that, regardless of temporary appearances, we live in a loving, supportive Universe. As Jesus said, we receive according to our faith.

# Two Worlds

*What was once called the objective world is a sort of Rorschach ink blot, into which each culture, each system of science and religion, each type of personality, reads a meaning only remotely derived from the shape and color of the blot itself.*— Lewis Mumford

*All that I see arises with my thoughts.*—Buddha

In choosing to see the world differently, it is helpful to remember that there are two worlds—the observable world of physical objects, and the underlying, nonobservable world described by physicists as energy and by philosophers and metaphysicians as thought or consciousness.

Both Jesus and the Sufis speak of being in this world but not of it. They are referring to living in the physical world of form and, at the same time, transcending physical appearances in our thought system and tuning in to the invisible world. In the Bible, Paul advised, *"Don't let the world around you squeeze you into its own mold, but let God remold your mind from within."* (Romans 12:2)

We can live in both worlds at the same time by consciously tuning in to the nonphysical sphere. We can be in the physical world and not of it by choosing to transcend the limiting concepts of the realm of appearances. This is our challenge: to see the world of appearances, to hear all the messages constantly emphasizing limitation and lack, and to choose to transcend this belief system and to see from a higher plane. This is an ongoing process. We choose, and then later we may notice that we have slipped back into the old way of seeing; if so, we choose again. Gradually our new expanded vision becomes a habit that replaces the old way of seeing and experiencing the world.

Jesus said, *"In the world you have tribulation . . . I have overcome the world."* (John 16:33) I think He was referring to the physical world of appearances, where we do experience tribulations and lack. We overcome that world by paying attention to the underlying world of limitlessness and wholeness.

My financial successes in real estate and the stock market were direct results of my being able to trust my intuition, which comes from that underlying world. Experiencing myself as part of an interconnected world helped me to feel less separate and alone, and this helped me trust. As I began to experience more deep trust in a safe and harmonious underlying world, I felt enabled to take risks.

My new level of trust opened the door to my asking Higher Power to assist me in attracting money so that I could support others. The result was similar to what some might describe as spiritual or religious faith. I would never have taken the risk on the stock market if I hadn't thoroughly believed in an underlying world that was quite different from the observable world of linear cause and effect.

When we experience the world as being interconnected, we don't feel so separate, with external things and people controlling us. Rather, we see that we are affecting what happens to us through our thoughts, which work on the level of invisible energy to attract experiences to us. When we believe that possibilities exist in the underlying world that seem unlikely or even weird in the everyday world of appearances, we begin to open the doors to perception of the nonphysical realm, thus allowing ourselves to see differently. This does not mean abandoning the rational approach. I test my intuition by applying my rational, logical mind: every step of the way, I check my expectations with the results and adjust course as necessary. It is an integration of both ways of knowing, and it takes some practice.

*Mind Training:*

## Seeing a Supportive World

This exercise is similar to the abundance switch. Whenever we notice ourselves feeling anxious, we can choose to feel differently. We can consciously shift into the trust-peace-joy feeling. We may have to "fake it until we make it," but when we have fully made the shift we experience the world as supportive.

I do not recommend that you force yourself to trust if you are in a situation that could be dangerous to your well-being. Use common sense. Anchor in the feeling of safety and supportedness in situations in which these responses come easily and no harm could happen to you, even if you are somewhat faking it.

For example, if you were feeling criticized at a meeting with some of your co-workers, you could consciously choose to feel that they were actually supporting you to make a change because they cared about you and your highest good.

To anchor in the feeling of being loved and supported, remember or imagine a situation in which you are surrounded by good friends or family members who love and support you. Look at their loving faces, receive their expressions of support, and soak in the peace and joy that is present when you allow yourself to feel loved and supported. Give these people back the same nurturing feelings. Savor the security of a mutual love and support system. (Some people use support groups, church gatherings, or workshops to access this feeling. For his support groups, Arnold Patent has designed an exercise in which each person takes a turn receiving the love and support of the group, so that all can learn to experience what it feels like.)

When you are experiencing the feeling of being loved and supported fully, take a couple of deep breaths and lightly press the fingers of your right hand into your palm. Feel the peace of being nurtured and supported. Do this again several times, feeling peace and trust in every cell in your body. Whenever you want to bring back this feeling, you can take a deep breath and press your fingers into your right palm, and the sensation will return.

You may also use the following visualization to anchor the feelings of being safe, nurtured, supported, and loved in a world that you can trust.

## Visualization: A Safe, Supportive World

*Get into a comfortable position and relax. Breathe in to a slow count of four, hold your breath, and breathe out to a slow count of four. Continue to do this ten times. Relax the muscles in your body.*

*Imagine that you are going for a walk in the woods. The day is warm and sunny. You feel the earth beneath your feet and hear a slight rustle as you step on old leaves and twigs. The trees surround your path until you come to a clearing. Sit down on the grass and look around and enjoy the beauty and peace of this place.*

*Notice the sun—always there to give you light and warmth. Even when there are clouds, the sun is still there waiting to share its light with you once again. Listen to the babbling brook happily bringing its nurturing water to you and others. Allow yourself to feel safe and nurtured in this beautiful place. The world is nurturing when we relax and attune ourselves with it. Allow yourself to feel secure and cared for. You are a beloved child of the Universe, and you are safe now and always. You are nurtured and loved. This is a caring Universe of love. You are loved and supported. Allow yourself to feel the love and support that is always there for you. This love and support will come to you when you relax. You can trust the Universe. You can relax and trust. Allow yourself to feel trust and to experience the deep peace and joy that comes with this feeling.*

*Take a couple deep breaths and lightly press your fingers into the palm of your right hand. Feel the peace of being nurtured and supported by the world. Do this again several times, feeling the peace and trust in every cell in your body. Still breathing deeply, see the sun shining its light to support you. Hear the brook murmuring its support of you. Feel the sun's warmth caressing you with love. When you want to bring back this feeling you can take a deep breath and press your fingers into your right palm, and the feeling will return.*

*Now tell yourself that in a moment you will feel wide awake and joyful, knowing that you are loved and supported. You will remember this feeling, and you can return to it whenever you choose.*

*Now slowly begin to move your fingers and toes. Move your body and remember where you are sitting. When you are ready, open your eyes. You are now wide awake and feeling joyful.*

# 10

## MASTERY OF INNER WEALTH AND POWER

*Let us think of life as a process of choices, one after another. At each point there is a progression choice and a regression choice. There may be a movement toward defense, toward safety, toward being afraid, but over on the other side there is the growth choice. To make the growth choice instead of the fear choice a dozen times a day . . . is a movement toward self-actualization.* —Abraham Maslow

*One's philosophy is not best expressed in words. It is expressed in the choices one makes. . . The process never ends until we die. And the choices we make are ultimately our responsibility.* —Eleanor Roosevelt

THIS CHAPTER introduces a five-step mastery process, which is a way of increasing our awareness of our implicit choices in life and of choosing again. It is not a quick fix. Nor does it require extraordinary ability. It does require commitment and practice.

Money freedom mastery comes from:

- Knowing that we are the source of our perception;
- Increasing our awareness of our thoughts, emotions, and choices; and
- Using the five steps to shift perception and choose again from the transformation state.

The mastery process is the steering device we use to correct our course as we move through uncharted land toward the goal of mastery. As we approach our goal, we are gradually learning that:

- We live in a space of unlimited possibility;
- There is no fixed reality, only interpretation;
- We are the source of power and wealth;
- Money is a tool and a mirror;
- Life is a learning experience, and the world is a feedback system;
- Mastery comes with choosing an interpretation that serves our highest purpose.

These realizations give us the courage to reach beyond our comfortable old behaviors and attitudes. As we release our attachment to the culturally agreed-upon reality, a higher perspective begins to emerge. This fresh perspective helps us make a leap into new territory—the kind of leap Sam Walton, of Wal-Mart, made in dreaming up a whole new way of merchandising; and that Anita Roddick took when she started the Body Shops, which sell natural products not tested on animals, parlaying a $7,000 investment into one of the world's most successful companies.

As we increasingly see ourselves and our world from the context of money freedom, we have choice and inner power. We don't feel threatened or displaced by a changing world; instead, we have the experience of being in the forefront of the new paradigm.

It is fun and exciting to be open, to welcome change. Life is an opportunity. When something isn't going well, we have the tools to shift it. We do not have to fear. We can go with the flow of life and be free.

## The Five-Step Mastery Process

1. HAVE CLEAR PURPOSE/INTENTION
2. OBSERVE NEUTRALLY
3. REFRAME MENTAL PERCEPTION
4. SHIFT YOUR FEELING STATE
5. ACT FROM THE TRANSFORMATION STATE

These steps operate both on the macro level of making paradigm shifts in our lives, and on the day-to-day micro level of reframing our immediate perceptions.

One client who made a paradigm shift was John, a starving artist. He was thirty-four and living at home because he couldn't support himself. His professors and other artist friends regarded him as talented. When I interviewed him, it was clear to me that he was being controlled by the false dilemma of feeling he had to choose between producing quality art and selling out.

*Step one* was for John to decide to find a way both to be true to his vision of painting and to make a living. He didn't really believe it was possible, but he made the commitment to be open to a new possibility.

*Step two* was for him to step outside his paradigm and observe his actions and thoughts neutrally. He began to notice his almost obsessive rejection of any suggestions about his art that might be construed as recommending "selling out." Gradually he realized that he was actually painting art that wouldn't sell in order to prove he was on the "correct" side of the either/or dilemma.

*Step three* involved shifting his paradigm so that it was an inclusive, "both/and" perspective. He chose to see that he could be true to his highest purpose of creating great art *and* to see money as a tool to support his work. This meant giving up his favorite pastime—judging and criticizing others for selling out, thus holding himself as superior to them. It is surprising how often we would rather be *right* than happy. John had to give up the payoff of being right in order to grow.

*Step four* entailed shifting his emotions regarding money, himself, and his view of the world. The visualizations, the NLP anchors, and the abundance switch outlined in this book are the tools for making this emotional shift. John had to experience inwardly feelings of worthiness, trust, and abundance before he was able to allow the shift in his outer life.

*Step five* was the shift into the transformation stage. John found himself seeing gallery owners as friends rather than as captives of the enemy—money. He could cooperate with them and allow himself to feel supported instead of standing alone against them. His paintings began to sell. Then gradually his painting style began to change: now his work is artistically as good as it was before, but more saleable. He still paints from his inner wisdom, but he can now hear this inner guidance more clearly.

When I last heard from John he was living in Paris, selling paintings, and enjoying life.

We can also use the five steps on a day-to-day basis. For instance, Janet wanted to apply for a new job in management. She was afraid she would be turned down, as she had been in the past. Her inner conversations revolved around fear of rejection. If she had applied for the job with that mind-set, she most probably would have gotten the expected rejection. However, by applying the five steps she consciously transformed her perspective of herself.

*Step one:* Janet chose to clarify her intention to work in management. She decided that this was really what she wanted to do.

*Step two:* Janet observed her attitude and self-talk from the stance of a neutral observer. She remembered how scared she had been when she applied for the other higher-level jobs and how she had never truly expected to get them. She realized that she didn't really believe that she was good enough to be a manager. She remembered the metaphysical law that we get what we expect.

*Step three:* She coached herself to put together a new story about herself, the job, and how qualified she was to get this position. She remembered all the activities that she had managed competently. She had a friend interview her, and she told him the new story of how she could do this job well. She practiced twice more with a tape recorder. She realized that she had to give up her payoff of staying small and safe in the old job and not having to grow.

*Step four:* Janet recognized that she had been anxious and fearful on the first two interviews and had thus blocked herself from seeing her own capabilities. This time she decided to shift her feelings about being a capable manager. She knew that if she felt shaky about her ability to handle the new job, the interviewers would pick that up. She did a visualization and reinforced her already existing anchor of abundance and of seeing the world as supporting her. Her practice with the anchor helped her to experience the confidence that she was already a good manager. She used the anchor before going in for the interview.

*Step five:* Janet moved herself into the transformation state. She found herself realizing that she really could do a good job in a managerial position. She allowed herself to sit quietly and listen to her own inner wisdom. A whole new perspective flooded in. She got in touch with a host of skills that she had forgotten she had. There came to mind incidents in her life in which she had done outstanding jobs of managing, as had happened with the school fair when her daughter was in second grade. She remembered everyone's praise for her work. Ideas about how she could excel in management occurred to her, and she saw new ways of making the position more effective.

Janet gave the interview from the transformation state, and she got the job.

Now let's examine each of the five steps in more detail.

## 1. Reinventing Your Life from Vision

*Some men see things as they are and say "Why?" I dream things that never were and say "Why not?"*— Robert F. Kennedy

*Clarity of intention leads to clarity of experience.*—Tom Carpenter, *Dialogue on Awakening*

*Hence first, in every experience, choose that which is to be the ideal; whether in the material world, the mental world, the spiritual world. For while one builds upon the other, and they become one in manifestation, there must be held that which is the standard, the criterion, the example to which one (or each) would attain.*

(1089-3)

Most people see their lives as being controlled by the past. But there is little possibility for improving our lives in the future if we are basing our attitudes and actions on the failures and limitations we have experienced in the past. Oprah Winfrey would not be the most popular and highest-paid entertainer if she had envisioned her future on the basis of childhood misfortunes. Nor would Maya Angelou have had the opportunity to read her poetry to the nation at a presidential inauguration if she had let the racial intimidation of her past define her potential.

We can stop allowing yesterday to control what we think is possible today. We needn't spend our time resisting the past. We can reverse the process and *create the present on the basis of a freely chosen future.* Instead of looking at the past and saying, *I can't have abundance because my parents brought me up wrong,* or *because I lack the schooling,* we can choose our vision of the future. We start with our vision, and work backward to figure out how to get there from where we are.

The United States put a man on the moon because Jack Kennedy created the vision that it was possible. He announced the vision when there was no concrete evidence that it could be realized. The scientists in NASA had to figure out how to make his vision a reality.

Once the vision is articulated and believed, the resources to make it possible begin to appear.

It is vital, however, to remember to create your vision out of the peace-trust-abundance state. When you envision the future from the anxiety-fear state, even the most desirable outcome has an ungrounded, unreal, wishful-thinking quality. So when you get ready to do the exercises described later in this chapter, be sure first to consciously shift to the peace-trust-abundance state.

Earlier in this book we saw how people's behavior is usually based on reactive, automatic responses from the unconscious mind. We saw the way in which the money myths of our society condition people's perceptions of wealth. We saw how the prevailing myth that circumstances are in charge of our lives keeps us from experiencing inner power.

Our most effective way of sabotaging our future is by saying to ourselves, "Yes, but in the past ... "

*Now it is time to be done with the past.*

You may want to do a completion exercise for your old jobs, for long-standing issues with money, or for relationships in which there is unfinished business. If you have any emotional charge about such things, there is still work to be done. In the completion exercise, express any unspoken thoughts or feelings about the issue. Talk to the people concerned, or use a friend or an empty chair as a surrogate for the person. Write a letter. It is okay not to mail the letter. The purpose of the exercise is to help you complete each experience so that you can remove the file from your active thoughts and from your subconscious, where it forms a block. It is helpful to reframe the situation so that the past is more supportive of your vision for the future. For instance:

Old thought:   *I'd love to start my own business, but I am afraid to because I failed the first time.*

Reframed thought:   *I can start a new business. The last business I had taught me what not to do, so now I can profit from that learning experience.*

Old thought:   *I'll never again tell the truth about what is going on for me, since that is how I got fired from my job.*

Reframed thought:   *I needed to leave my past job. On some level I got myself fired to give me the push I needed.*

Reframe anything in the past that is holding you back. Then declare, *THE PAST IS DEAD.* Declare, *I ACCEPT LIFE AS A CLEAN SLATE ON WHICH I CAN WRITE A NEW STORY FOR MY LIFE.*
You may want to do a little ceremony. Write the story of the past on sheets of paper. Write as much as you want to. Now take the papers and build a fire and burn them. Bury the ashes or throw them into a river. Let the past go lovingly, for if there is anger, it will chain you to your former life. Release the past as the determinant of your present and future. Thank it for its service and declare it finished. Take a stand to create a new life based on your conscious choice. Now is the time. You can declare yourself in charge of your life. Make the declaration and step into a new life.
Give yourself an academy award for the old movie, called *Your Life,* and begin a new movie. In the old movie you were the actor. The past, your subconscious, and your external circumstances were the writer and director. In the new movie, make yourself the writer, director, actor, and neutral observer. You are the source of what happens in your life. You choose how you will interpret your life, no matter what you were born into.
Helen Keller was born into what would appear to most people as great misfortune, since she was deaf, blind, and unable to speak. She became an outstanding teacher by her refusal to accept herself as the victim of her physical disability.
Victor Frankl used his experience as a concentration camp inmate in Germany to learn fundamental truths about the human condition—insights he later wrote and taught to others. When we see our life as a learning oppor-

tunity, our circumstances become part of the learning. We are the learner, and we are the source of our interpretation.

We open unlimited possibilities by designing our present using the future we choose. The secret is to *give ourselves permission* to be big enough to follow our purpose.

Ask yourself the following questions. For each one, write down the first answer that pops into your mind, as you want to access the intuitive mind, not the analytical left brain. You may want to put yourself in a meditative state before asking the questions. If you aren't satisfied with the answers, you can use the technique taught earlier of asking the question using the dominant hand and answering with the nondominant hand.

- What do I desire to do with my life?
- What is my higher purpose?
- What would I do with my life if I had all the money I could possibly use?
- What do I want to be remembered for? What would I want said about myself in my epitaph?

*Exercise*

## What is Your Purpose?

One way to expand your vision is to keep asking the same question over and over. This can be done alone; it is even more effective if you do it with a friend who agrees to repeat the question a minimum of ten times.

Remember to put yourself in the peace-trust-love state before beginning the exercise.

What is your purpose?
What is your purpose?
What is your purpose?

Create a vision of yourself fulfilling your purpose *now.*

Step inside your vision and *become* it. Say to yourself, for example:

*I am doing outstanding work empowering poor and homeless people, and money is pouring in to support me generously.*
*I am organizing international children's concerts with an abundance of volunteer and financial support.*

Sometimes the purpose statement works better if we give it a longer time frame. For example:

*By a year from now (use actual date) I am successfully following my purpose and being abundantly supported.*
*By a year from now I am fully accepting my identity as a successful entrepreneur, and I'm experiencing financial abundance.*

It is more powerful to make the vision real as of now by saying *I am* than to see it in the future and say *I will.* The subconscious mind operates in the present. To communicate effectively with the subconscious mind, so that it assists us, we must speak in the present tense.

Say and write your purpose in the present, as in the examples:

*My purpose is* _____ .

Choose your purpose. Make a commitment to it. Reinvent your interpretation of events in the context of your purpose.

## 2. Being the Neutral Observer

*The process of witnessing is dispassionate. It's not committed to one result or another; it's open to everything . . . it is more able to see the truth.*—Ram Dass & Paul Gorman, *How Can I Help?*

Being our own neutral observer or self-witness creates a new context for living. We develop an awareness of what we are doing that allows us to break free of automatic reactive responses. We gain new eyes to see a wider version of "reality." Witnessing means observing from a place of nonattachment. This allows us to see truth. We can know that the way we are experiencing ourselves and our situation is just a result of our perception. We remember that we have the freedom to shift paradigms.

The important thing is not to let the internal critic sneak into the role of the observer. When we allow ourselves to judge, then the whole process becomes stuck.

In case you are tempted to beat up on yourself for being a captive of your old paradigms, here are some quotations from famous people who, at one time or another, became stuck in an old-paradigm view. These passages are taken from Joel Barker's book, *Future Edge: Discovering the New Paradigms of Success:*

*The phonograph ... is not of any commercial value.*
—Thomas Edison, to his assistant, 1880

*Sensible and responsible women do not want to vote.*
—Grover Cleveland, 1905

*I think there is a world market for about five computers.*—Thomas J. Watson, chairman of IBM, 1943

*There is no reason for any individual to have a computer in their home.*—Ken Olsen, president of Digital Equipment Corporation, 1977

We are in good company when we are stuck in our paradigms. Most new inventions—from the steamboat ("Fulton's folly"), to Land's polaroid camera, to Xerox photography—have been laughed at or ignored because they didn't fit into an existing worldview. We don't accept as possible that which lies outside our paradigm. As society resists paradigm shifts, we do the same in our personal lives.

The important thing is simply to observe what is going on, knowing that our own discomfort is part of the natural process of change and transformation.

*Exercise*

## The Observer Exercise

This is an excellent exercise for increasing your awareness, or observer consciousness.

Each night, recount all the limited-self, negative thoughts that you have had all day. Start with the most recent thought and work backward to the morning. Take each thought and transform it into a loving, empowered thought or statement. In time, you will find yourself becoming more aware of your thoughts and statements. You may want to jot down your limiting thoughts as you go along during the day, so that you can remember them for the evening exercise. Notice the pattern of the thoughts. *Do this exercise without judging yourself.* If you do judge yourself in any way, count that as a thought to be transformed in the evening exercise.

## 3. Creating Your Own Paradigm Shifter

*What is impossible to do in your_____, but if it could be done, would fundamentally change it?*—Joel Arthur Barker, *Future Edge: Discovering the New Paradigms of Success*

What is your self-paradigm in relation to wealth and power? What do you think is impossible? What is the game of life as you see it? What are its rules? How could you rewrite the game and its rules?

Barker calls the following question his "paradigm shifting" question. He uses it with businesses, but you can apply
it just as effectively to your personal life.

*What is impossible for you to do, given your current rela-
tionship with wealth and power, but if it could be done,
would fundamentally change that relationship?*

The word "impossible" nearly always signals an unconscious assumption that is part of the lens through which
you are seeing the world. The word "fundamentally" means
that the change does not take place *within* your old mental
framework. You must go *beyond* that framework.

One of the requirements for making a personal paradigm
shift is that you trust your intuition—that you trust yourself. Another is that you be able to look at situations from
new perspectives. We must be able to project a part of our
consciousness "outside" ourselves in order to observe our
own assumptions and behaviors from a novel viewpoint.
The more we practice using our intuition and our "outside
observer" to try out new perspectives and to reframe how
we see things, the more we come to trust the process of self-
transformation.

According to Barker, in business it is the outsider who
most often brings about valuable paradigm shifts. The outsider doesn't fully recognize the assumptions under which
the group is operating and doesn't have a vested interest in
maintaining the status quo. Some people, like Einstein at
the time he was formulating the Special Theory of Relativity, are outsiders by virtue of youthful innocence.

Thus arises the importance of maintaining a personal
observer, who is an outsider relative to your own self-paradigm. Allow your observer to ask "dumb" questions, to
reframe the way you interpret situations, to view your world
as would someone from another planet or from a radically
different culture.

My experience with money is outside the prevailing paradigm, which is why I told it in such detail. I didn't accept the

assumption that it is hard to make a living following a divorce. I didn't buy the programming that said I should work long hours, struggle, and go back to school. I did study, but not the program prescribed by the mainstream paradigm. I didn't get another degree in the old paradigm.

I chose to reinvent my self-paradigm. Once we make the leap of letting go of our old, apparently secure boundaries, it is fun to accept new challenges. It takes courage, but it is rewarding.

As Helen Keller once said, "Life is either a daring adventure or nothing at all."

## 4. Shifting Your Feeling State

The reason affirmations often don't work for people is that the person making them doesn't shift the feeling state. If we are stating our mental intention to experience abundance to support us, and at the same time we are feeling anxious and distrustful, the feeling state will override the affirmation.

In chapter 7 we saw how to shift the feeling state by using the NLP anchor, the abundance switch, and the abundance visualization. Go back and review the chapter and use those tools to consciously shift to the peace-joy-abundance state.

It is helpful when contemplating an action to ask, What feeling state will this action produce? Will this action bring me inner peace? Will it put me in a state of peace-joy-abundance? Is this action consistent with that state? If not, then it is time to begin the process again. In doing so you may find that a different course is appropriate, or that you need to change your perception of what the contemplated action is for.

It is often more important to examine the reason for taking a particular course than to analyze the action itself. For example, if I am planning to cancel a proposed business project in order to get even with my partner, the action is not appropriate. In that case, it would be helpful to stop and do the mastery process, and then to make a decision from a new perspective that serves my highest good. If, on the other hand, I am planning to cancel because I feel that the project is going to be a bad experience for both of us, then the action is appropriate. The way that I cancel in the second scenario will be different, and it will leave the door open for another project that may be highly profitable for both of us.

## 5. The Transformation State

*The primary wisdom is intuition. In that deep force, the last fact behind which analysis cannot go, all things find their common origin ... We live in the lap of immense intelligence. We are the receivers of its truth and organs of its activity.*—Ralph Waldo Emerson

*My first bid, hastily made, was $165,000. Then somehow that didn't feel right to me. Another figure kept coming, $180,000. It satisfied me. It seemed fair. It felt right. I changed my bid to the larger figure on that hunch. When they were opened, the closest bid to mine was $179,800. I got the Stevens Corporation by a narrow margin of $200.00. Eventually the assets returned me $2 million.*—Conrad Hilton

*His expert consultant advised him not to buy the restaurants. He said he fumed and then called his lawyer and said to take it. His explanation: I felt in my funny bone it was a sure thing.*—said of Ray Kroc, on his buying McDonald's

*I run the company on instinct, I'm an instinct player, an instinct actor, and I use it to guide me in business.*—Oprah Winfrey, top-paid businesswoman and entertainer

In the transformation state we are open to access our inner wisdom, or intuition. That intuition has been present all along, but ordinarily we are unable to tell when it is the voice of inner wisdom that is speaking, and when it is merely wishful thinking. After all, we all know people who have ungrounded, grandiose ideas that never amount to anything.

A crucial difference is that wishful thinking and grandiose ideas come from the anxiety-fear state, while intuition comes from the seat of peace-love-abundance, which is closely related to the transformation state. Therefore, as we move into the transformation state the doors of intuition open wide before us.

The transformation state is the place of unlimited possibilities. It is the state wherein we access inner wisdom, creativity, inspiration, imagination, insight, vision, talent, guidance, the divine spirit within, and breakthroughs that totally defy the old context or paradigm. This is the place from which Einstein achieved his breakthrough on relativity, Mozart composed his symphonies, Steven Jobs invented the Apple computer, and Oprah Winfrey created a new type of talk show.

According to Weston Agor, author of *Intuitive Management: Integrating Left and Right Brain Management Skills*, psychological tests on more than 2,000 business managers showed that *effective managers rely most heavily on their feelings and intuition* when they make their most important decisions.

The transformation state frees up the part of us that sees from a larger context. Our problems are products of our little, habitual, conditioned self. Discovering our expanded Self is like climbing to a mountaintop overlooking the foggy valley in which we created the problems.

When Einstein said that we cannot solve a problem at the level at which it was created, he was telling us to rise up to a new level—the transformation state. If a person has gotten into debt because of a personal paradigm according to which life is stacked against her, she will not solve the problem by getting a second job at night. The pattern will just reappear, since it reflects her underlying mind-set and emotional state. The problem can be solved in the long term by using the five steps outlined earlier in this chapter to come into the transformation state. From that place, she can get into a totally new job field or start a business that will support her well, and not merely pay off the old debt.

The transformation state helps us to see in a context of wider possibility and to assess situations and feedback more accurately. It gives us new eyes so that we see from an empowered perspective that the world is loving and supportive of us.

The transformation state is the cumulative result of the four steps that have gone before. When we are in it, we perceive and act from our inner source. We can make extraordinary leaps of discovery and insight that weren't possible from our previous state. From this place of inner knowing, we have the courage to act, even when our action may appear to others not to make sense. The courage of our convictions comes from our inner knowing.

## Using the Mastery Process

When we are stuck, we are holding fast to a way of perceiving the world that does not empower and support us. But we always have the opportunity to *choose to see the situation differently*. That is the source of inner power. We can choose to shift our perception of a situation to one that sets us free to have what we desire in life.

In high school my son, Evan, went through an unpleasant period during which he accumulated speeding tickets. He had to listen to his parents' lectures, pay the extra insurance premium, and spend days watching accident movies provided by the local department of motor vehicles.

Evan went to college in our home state while he was still on probation as the result of his driving. He attended Virginia Tech, where many students felt superior to the "townie" cops; the police, in return, resented the students. After his first run-in with the police, Evan was facing the prospect of losing his license if he got another ticket. He made the decision to stay free of driving tickets.

In addition to the commitment to driving more carefully, he consciously chose to see the police differently. Instead of being angry at them, which attracted them to act out his expectation that they would "get" him, he decided to send them love and appreciation. He shifted to seeing them as people who believed they were doing their duty and who had jobs to do in order to earn a living and feed their families. He reframed both his mental picture and his feeling state. It worked!

A couple, Jappy and Kathy Becker, were driving home from the movies with their two children when a car that was drag racing swerved into their van and killed their fourteen-year-old daughter, Loren. The hit-and-run driver turned out to be a seventeen-year-old boy, Jorge deJesus, who ran away from the accident scene because he was terrified.

After Jorge was apprehended, Kathy received a call from the prosecutor's office asking what punishment she recommended under the provisions of the state victim's rights law. She asked for more information about Jorge. The official said that at that moment the boy was curled up in a fetal position, rocking and unable to lift up his head. He could only manage to whisper, and he said that he wished he could exchange his life for Loren's.

Kathy later described her reaction: "Suddenly, I felt a mother's compassion for this emotionally devastated boy. I saw no enemy, no culprit, just a heartbroken child who was frightened and alone."

To the official she said, "Tell him I forgive him." Then she experienced a huge burden being lifted from her shoulders.

Kathy went on to enter a supportive relationship with Jorge as he served a sentence that was shortened because of her intervention. As a result of this shift in perception to seeing him with compassion instead of anger, her whole life changed. Both Kathy and her husband went through a deep spiritual transformation. They are now living more fulfilled lives, and their relationships have deepened.

A major shift in perception on the mental and emotional planes can change our lives in dramatic ways. We all can create this kind of shift for ourselves.

*Exercise*

## Creating from the Future

This exercise can be used to practice the five-step mastery process. It is done best with another person, so that one of you can ask the other the questions. Alternatively, it can be done with an imaginary person sitting in an empty chair across from you. Or it can be done in writing.

Imagine yourself five years in the future, having achieved wealth and inner power. You are living your vision successfully and joyously. You are feeling good about yourself and your accomplishments over the last five years. You are about to share this experience with your friend. Be sure to fill in lots of detail and *feel* the reality of your story. Your friend says:

*Tell me about your life now, since I haven't seen you in five years.*

*You seem so happy. How did this all come about?*

*What did you do to change your life? What were the specific steps you took? (Here is the opportunity to go through the five steps, which will help you practice remembering and experiencing them.)*

*How did this progression take place?*

*What accomplishments along the way made it possible for you to make the next major step?*

*What advice do you have for me to enable me to do the same thing with my life?*

You can do this exercise as many times as you like, both with day-to-day activities, as Janet did when she applied for a new job, and with major paradigm shifts. Let your imagination run loose and play. If this is done with a light attitude, you can open more possibilities.

Reinventing our lives is an art, not an exact science. It is an ongoing process, and we increase our confidence, expertise, and skill as we practice it. Relax and enjoy the process.

# 11

## GRADUATION—FROM FROG TO PRINCE

*Once the self-concept changes, behavior changes to match the newly perceived self.* —Carl Rogers

*For unto everyone that hath [the consciousness] shall be given and he shall have abundance.* —Matthew 25:29

*Every great religion claims that our suffering is the product of ignorance and illusion. Suffering, they say, results when we forget who we really are—Children of God, Atman, Buddha Nature or one with the Tao—and mistake ourselves for limited being, skin-encapsulated egos trapped inside fragile, transitory bodies. We suffer ultimately, say the great religions, from a case of mistaken identity, a false self-concept, an erroneous image that is but a pale shadow of our true limitless being.*
—Francis Vaughan and Roger Walsh,
*A Gift of Healing: Selections from* A Course in Miracles

*LITTLE, LIMITED SELF:* I feel alone and anxious about getting enough money.

*GREATER, WHOLE SELF:* I am an extension of infinite mind, a whole being, connected and related to all, and wealth flows in as a reflection of my inner wealth.

*LESSON:* I can expand my identity from being the drop in the ocean to being the ocean, with all its resources.

Thank you   Thank you   Thank you   Thank you   Thank you
Thank you   Thank you   Thank you   Thank you   Thank you
Thank you   Thank you   Thank you   Thank you   Thank you
Thank you   Thank you   Thank you   Thank you   Thank you
Thank you   Thank you   Thank you   Thank you   Thank you
Thank you   Thank you   Thank you   Thank you   Thank you

READ THE words with feeling. Say "Thank you" and really mean it for five minutes, and see how it makes you feel. You can't feel scarcity while you are expressing gratitude. We feel either one or the other. Feeling grateful is a good way to jump from the little, empty self to the Whole, full self.

Our experience of wealth and inner power is blocked when we see ourselves as small, isolated, victimized, and conditioned by the past. The little self, almost by definition, rejects parts of itself. When we deny or reject, we block the free flow of abundance energy. When we expand our identity—when we identify with our Whole Self—we set ourselves free and allow ourselves to experience the unlimited flow of energy from our source. The Whole Self is by definition complete, not lacking, uninjured. It is the essential wholeness we are before we learn fear and scarcity and conditioned love. It is the spiritual or soul part of us, which is an extension of the unlimited Universe—the source of wealth, power, love, happiness, security, peace, and fulfillment.

This is not about *achieving* the Whole Self or *achieving* abundance. It is about removing the blocks to experiencing the Whole Self and abundance, which already exist. When we shift our identity to the Whole Self, we open ourselves to receive and experience our inner and outer riches. Imagine being Superman or Wonder Woman, and stepping into a phone booth to pull off the outer clothes of the little-self identity, revealing the true self—the all-powerful Whole Self, a force for good—concealed within.

Another way of describing this transformation is to say that the journey from one identity to the other amounts to substituting our unlimited Prince identity for our little frog identity. Problems with regard to money will then transform themselves. This transformation from little self to Whole Self, from frog to prince, is your graduation from the school of money freedom.

We all know the fairy tale in which the princess kisses the frog and turns him into a prince. Every fairy tale has an important message. In this case, it is that each of us has a prince within us. The story implies that it is possible for us to substitute one identity for another. The revelation of the noble person within is not a matter of giving up bad habits or striving to be a better frog. *It is a jump from one identity to another.*

In an another fairy tale, a girl named Cinderella lives as the victim of her stepmother and stepsisters, forced to clean the house and to do chores all day. Her fairy godmother enables her to experience a wonderful new identity, in which she is recognized as the most beautiful girl in the kingdom. At midnight, Cinderella reverts to her old, limited identity, but in time she is rescued by the prince and leaves her charwoman self behind for good.

The mean stepmother and stepsisters in this story represent our own beliefs and feelings that keep us imprisoned. The prince is not merely a handsome and powerful man who will rescue us. If we take the story literally in that regard, we may live a life of illusion and disappointment. The rescuer is actually a part of ourselves that we are capable of summoning. I call this part the outside observer, who sees beyond the limited viewpoint of the little self and thereby sets us free to become our Greater, Whole Self. Occasionally we forget and slide back into our little, limited identity; then we again summon our outside observer to help us be the free and beautiful Whole Self. When we expand into our Whole Self, then wealth, inner power, peace, and fulfillment flow naturally into our lives.

My financial success story, which I related in chapter 1, wasn't really about making money. It was about finding my Whole Self. It was about my experience of learning the self-empowerment process, which substitutes the Whole Self for the little self. You can do this, too.

# A Case of Mistaken Identity

*Imagine a person who suddenly wakes up in a hospital after a road accident to find she is suffering from total amnesia. Outwardly, everything is intact; she has the same face and form, her senses and her mind are there, but she doesn't have any idea or any trace of a memory of who she really is. In exactly the same way, we cannot remember our true identity, our original nature. Frantically, and in real dread, we cast around and improvise another identity . . . This false and ignorantly assumed identity is the "ego."—*Sogyal Rimpoche, *The Tibetan Book of Living and Dying*

*At a very early age you begin to form the core of the ego's addictive thought system: that you are fundamentally inadequate as you are, and need something outside of yourself to make you whole . . . It is the denial of our underlying wholeness that is the foundation of addiction.—*Lee Jampolsky, Ph.D., *Healing the Addictive Mind*

The caterpillar thinks that caterpillar is her total identity. She has no idea that there is a potential butterfly in her. Like the caterpillar, we suffer from a case of mistaken identity, which is the condition of not knowing that there is a Whole Self into which we can transform ourselves.

Two people have been living in you all your life—the little, limited self (the ego); and the Whole Self, the Greater Abundant Self, the Spiritual Self, which has innate wisdom and power and abundance.

Deepak Chopra has written that in all the cases he knows of in which people have cured themselves of supposedly "incurable" diseases, there was a shift in consciousness where the person experienced an expanded identity, realizing that they were part of a larger whole. This is true as well for all the people I personally know who have cured themselves of cancer and heart disease.

Most of us share a mistaken perception of who we are. We see ourselves as a little, separate self that has to strive to make it; that has to compete to get its share; that has to control or be controlled; that has to struggle to get love, money, and power; that is not good enough; that either makes it in a situation or fails; that is afraid (even if the fear is denied and projected outward so that one sees others as threatening); that somehow has to get security from an external source; that is trying to *get there*, however "there" is defined; that is lacking in something.

This mistaken perception of who we are comes from the fact that we tend to identify with our body rather than with our essence. When we look at ourselves in the mirror, we see only a reflection of our physical shell; we see the picture frame of our being, but not the picture itself—the package, not the contents. The body, for all its miraculous qualities and abilities, is limited in space and time; it has a certain size and weight, and it appears to be distinct from other bodies and from its surroundings. But these are not the qualities of the unlimited Whole Self.

The ancient sages attributed fear to the feeling of separateness and to the tendency to see the world in terms of dualities, beginning with the duality of "me" and "not-me." Since fear is the principal block to allowing abundance to flow into our lives, it is easy to see how the mistaken identification of the Self with its body—which is the root of our fears—may be the real source of any inability to experience fulfillment in life.

Separation is an illusion of the senses. Quantum physics shows us that we are in fact interpenetrating waves of energy. The science of ecology makes it clear that we are part of an interconnected living system. Philosophers, mystics, and spiritual teachers have repeatedly told us that we are all spiritually one. Yet we tend steadfastly to cling to the illusion that we are separate, isolated egos, competing against one another for a limited supply of goods.

We know that our physical senses respond to only a small portion of the total energy spectrum. We can't see, touch, smell, or hear the electromagnetic waves that our television sets receive and transform into pictures and sound. We can't see the x-rays in the doctor's and dentist's office.

And even with regard to the energy we *can* perceive, we are often subject to illusions or misperceptions. The sun appears to go up and down, but we know that this is only an appearance. The sun appears to be gone on a rainy day, but it is still there behind the clouds.

Likewise when it comes to the sun of our own Self, we often allow clouds of illusion to darken our vision. We stubbornly cling to a mistaken identity of limitation and separateness regardless of the cost. Indeed, we often become so attached to our illusions of separateness that we refuse to recognize the truth of oneness even when it knocks on our door.

The Buddha knew this tendency well and described it in the following story:

A young widower had a five-year-old son whom he loved dearly. One day while he was away on business, robbers burned his village to the ground and kidnapped his son. When the man returned, he was distraught and took the charred remains of another child to be those of his son. He performed a cremation ceremony and put the ashes in a beautiful bag, which he kept with him at all times.

One day the man's real son escaped from the robbers and came back to the village. He arrived at his father's new home at midnight, knocked on the door, and called out to his father. However, his father was still so distraught with his loss that he could not recognize his own son's voice. He assumed some mischie-

vous child was making fun of him, so he told the boy to
go away; meanwhile, he continued to cry. The son
knocked again and again and pleaded with his father
to let him in, but to no avail. Finally the child left. The
father and son never saw each other again.

After telling this story, the Buddha reputedly said,
*Some time, somewhere, you take some idea or belief to
be the truth. If you cling to it too strongly, then when the
truth comes in person and knocks at your door, you will
not open it.*

Virtually all human problems on both the societal and
personal levels can be traced back to our root belief that we
are separate from everything else. It is an idea (valid at a
certain level of experience) which we have clung to so des-
perately that we refuse to hear the truth that is knocking at
our door. Our misassumption leads to fear, greed, lack, con-
tention, and all the other blocks to our experience of peace,
harmony, abundance, and inner power.

The Latin root of the word *scarce* means "to pluck out" or
"to separate." We create scarcity in our personal lives and in
the larger world because we separate ourselves, we pluck
ourselves from the universal context of abundance.

Dr. Lee Jampolsky, in his book *Healing the Addictive
Mind*, defines addiction as "pursuing happiness in things
(people, places, substances) external to myself." By that
definition, our little self is the quintessential addict. The
little, limited self comes from the premise that *I lack* something and must get it from the external world if I am to be
okay. This leads to the anxious striving for more and more, a
hunger that never can be satisfied.

## Abundance and Inner Power—
## By-products of the Greater, Whole Self

*Within the framework of the physical experience you*

*may create as much abundance as you desire ... The ability you have to create this abundance stems from your true creative capacities as an infinite Being... The thing that will be manifest in your physical consciousness has no value. The fact that you can manifest/create it and that this manifestation bears a parallel to the true expression of your Being does have value.*—Tom Carpenter, *Dialogue on Awakening*

The shift to the Greater, Whole Self is a quantum leap into a new paradigm of selfhood. We begin to operate from a new set of assumptions and possibilities. Since my perception of the world reflects my paradigm filters, I begin to see a different world. Limitation and lack begin to disappear from my external world as they disappear from my inner world. The little-self experience of being controlled by circumstances, people, and things is transformed by the Whole Self, who knows that *it* is the source of inner power.

Everything flows from the self-concept. When I am my limited self, I see a limited world of lack and struggle. When I make the quantum leap into the expanded consciousness of my abundant Whole Self, the world has made the same quantum leap in its appearance to me. It is like seeing the world shift from black and white to vibrant colors. This is not an incremental change. The Greater, Whole Self is an experience of *unlimited* love, abundance, inner peace, inner power, joy, and harmony.

The Whole Self knows that I am enough and that I have enough. The Whole Self knows its connection to Source or Higher Power and knows that the infinite "enough" comes from within. One is always *giving*, as one is always full. Just as giving love expands the love we receive, so all giving expands our receiving. What we give, we give to ourselves, as all is interconnected.

*Our little self is:*

coming from emptiness and lack
seeking to get from the external world
fear-based
controlled by habits and past conditioning
limited
separate and judging
convinced the world isn't safe
stuck on either/or

*Our Whole Self is:*

coming from infinite fullness and wholeness
giving from an inner abundance
love-based
in the present
unlimited
interconnected part of the whole, and accepting
sure the world is safe and supportive
focused on both/and
inspired, imaginative, intuitive, creative, and knowing
paradigm shifting
capable of leaps of brilliance
connected to Infinite Intelligence
an extension of the Creator's perfection
expressing inner wealth and power
characterized by abundance, joy, and inner peace
our Spiritual, Whole Self

*When we are the Greater, Whole Self, abundance and inner power show up as by-products of who we are.*
    When we see ourselves as the Whole Self, we are part of an interconnected living system. Abundance is abundance for all, when we are interconnected. We are full and unlimited, a part of the cosmic dance of life. We are connected

into a level of imagination and intelligence that is limitless.

Edward M. Forester, who did some of the seminal writing on creativity, said, "In the creative state a man is taken out of himself. He lets down . . . a bucket into his subconscious, and draws up something which is normally beyond his reach. He mixes this thing with his normal experiences, and out of the mixture he makes a work of art."

The music that Mozart wrote as a child of ten could not have come from the limited consciousness of the little self. He already knew how to access the infinite intelligence available to the Whole Self. Many of Einstein's remarks show clearly that he too knew how to shift his identity from the little self to the Whole Self. Indeed, all of the intuitive breakthroughs of scientists, inventors, and business people give evidence of the Whole Self's intuitive creativity.

In our little-self identity we are like a group of people sitting in a sparsely furnished room complaining about lack. Above them is a trap door that is tightly fastened shut. Above the trap door is unlimited abundance waiting to flow through to them. However, their conditioned habits keep them from even looking up and noticing the trap door. All that is needed is the shift to the Greater, Whole Self, with the openness to receive and the expanded wisdom to see and open the door.

The shift to the Whole Self is like turning on a light. The electricity was in your house all the time, but you had to choose to flip the switch to allow the light to shine. When we are in our little-self identity, we unconsciously resist receiving, and we sabotage ourselves. When we shift into the Whole Self, we open ourselves to receive and turn on the light switch.

Choose to receive abundance by turning the switch to your Whole-Self identity. That is what I believe Jesus was saying when He said, "Seek ye first the Kingdom of Heaven and all else will be added unto you." The Kingdom of Heaven is a state of consciousness.

*Exercise*

## Turn Up the Intensity on the Whole-Self Outlook

At the end of chapter 3, I introduced the exercise on Changing the Intensity. You can use that technique to increase the intensity with which you experience the Whole-Self outlook and turn down the intensity with which you experience the limited-self outlook.

When beliefs, feelings, or memories come up that are characteristic of the anxious, limiting self, remove yourself from them. Make them small, dim, fuzzy, dull, uninteresting, still, colorless, distant, and silent. Step outside them and see them from afar, as if you were viewing them from a mountaintop or through someone else's eyes. Make them a movie that you are observing without involvement.

When the thoughts, perceptions, and feelings of the Whole Self come up, increase their intensity. Make them loud, big, bright, vivid, close at hand, dynamic, clear, and moving. Step inside the experience and be there. See, hear, and feel it happening to you now.

*Exercise*

## Whole-Self Visualization and Anchor

*Find a peaceful place, sit down, and make yourself comfortable. Let go and relax. Take a deep breath, hold it, and let it out slowly. Continue exhaling even after it seems that all the breath is gone. Do this five times.*

*Feel the muscles in your shoulders let go and relax. Feel the muscles in your neck let go and relax. Feel the muscles in your face relax. Open your jaw and feel the jaw muscles relax.*

*Now imagine that you are sitting on the sand at the edge of the ocean or a lake. You can hear the rhythm of the waves*

*lapping the shore. The temperature is pleasant, a* 
*comfortable. The sun is shining on you. You look* 
*joy the cloudless blue sky. The sun is bright. You feel* ~~the so,~~ 
*sand under you as you shift position to be fully comfortable.*

*You begin to feel your body expanding. Gradually you are* 
*growing larger and larger. The borders of your body are get-* 
*ting fuzzy, and your energy continues to expand. You are ex-* 
*panding to encompass the whole beach. Now you are* 
*encompassing the water too. It feels good to be expanding.* 
*You are feeling like energy that can expand indefinitely. You* 
*feel light. You are feeling a blissful joy. You are feeling free and* 
*full. You know that you are the Greater, Whole Self, an expres-* 
*sion of the infinite wholeness of the universe. You are part of* 
*the cosmic dance. You are interconnected and related to ev-* 
*erything, and it is a joyous state.*

*You look down at the beach and see the wide expanse of* 
*white sand and blue water. It is so beautiful. See the spar-* 
*kling reflections of the sun on the water below you. Look* 
*down on your physical body, your little self, sitting there on* 
*the beach. You are filled with compassion for that person.* 
*You are full of love for your little self. You feel like the sun,* 
*beaming infinite energy down on your little self. You know* 
*that you are the infinite source of joy, happiness, and abun-* 
*dance for your little self.*

*Tell your little self: "I love you far beyond your capacity to* 
*imagine. I am always here to support you. You can call upon* 
*me any time. I am your source. I am beaming love down on* 
*you now so that you can have some sense of the feeling of* 
*infinite love. You can have all the abundance and inner* 
*power you want by tuning in to me. And material abundance* 
*in itself isn't what is important. What is important is that* 
*you experience me, your Whole Self, as your being. Once you* 
*remove the blocks, my energy will flow into your body. I am* 
*like the electricity in your house—invisible, but available any* 
*time you flip the switch. When you listen and ask, I will an-* 
*swer. When you surrender your little identity to my unlim-*

*ited one, you will experience me, your Greater, Whole Self.
When you leave your mind open, I will guide your life from
this expanded perspective. I desire for you to live a full, joyous, abundant life. Like Aladdin's genie, I am here to serve
you, my beloved little self. I am the wholeness and interconnectedness that you have forgotten. I love and accept you always. We are one."*

*Now gradually begin to make yourself smaller. Feel your-
self slowly returning to the boundaries of your physical body.
Relax into the body, feeling refreshed and vibrant. Assist the
little self to feel both itself and you—the Greater, Whole Self.*

*With the little self, take several deep breaths; have the little
self press the body's fingers into the palm of the right hand.*

*I am speaking to the little self now: Feel the joy of also be-
ing the expanded Whole Self. You are an extension of the infinite love of creation. Feel your expanded Self and the infinite
love that the Whole Self has for you. Still taking deep breaths
and pressing together the fingers and the palm of the body's
right hand, tune in to the joy and expanded feeling that you
are experiencing. Hear the sound of the waves on the shore.
See the brilliance of the sun sparkling on the water. When
you want to bring back this feeling, you can do so by taking a
deep breath and pressing the fingers of your right hand into
your palm.*

*Know that you can return to this feeling of the Whole Self
any time you choose. You can feel your expanded being and
let it help you. All you have to do is relax, take a deep breath,
and press together your right hand.*

*Now tell yourself that in a moment you will feel wide
awake and refreshed, with new energy. You will remember
the joyful, expanded feeling of the Whole Self. You will be able
to connect with that part of yourself whenever you choose.*

*Now slowly begin to move your fingers and feet. Remem-
ber where you are and what you are wearing. When you are
ready, open your eyes. You are wide awake and feeling good.*

## The Shift Technique

*I am willing to see this differently. I am willing to remember who I am.*—A Course in Miracles

*More and more, then, instead of the harsh and fragmented gossip that ego has been talking to you all your life, you will find yourself hearing in your mind the clear directions of the teachings, which inspire, admonish, guide, and direct you at every turn. The more you listen, the more guidance you will receive. If you follow the voice of your wise guide, the voice of your discriminating awareness, and let ego fall silent, you come to experience that presence of wisdom and joy and bliss that you really are.*—Sogyal Rimpoche, *The Tibetan Book of Living and Dying*

Olympic athletes achieve mastery by intention, commitment, and practice. Likewise, we can obtain mastery of inner power and abundance by intention, commitment, and practice. The shift technique does not require any special ability or talents. We can all do it if we so choose.

The shift technique is a retraining exercise for the mind and the feeling state. We use it to retrain our mind as an athlete would retrain her body. She would practice; notice what she was doing wrong; choose again, to do it differently this time; and practice doing it differently. Likewise, in the shift technique we notice when we are coming from our limited, habitual, little self; and we choose again, to come from our Whole Self and Inner Wisdom. This is similar to the mastery process described in chapter 10.

The shift technique is a breath-intentionality process that helps us shift our identity to that of our Whole Self. While breathing in deeply and holding our breath, we silently speak our intention to be our Whole Self; at the same time, we visualize and feel ourself as the Whole Self.

During the in breath, see yourself filling up with or full of love and abundance. On the out breath, see yourself experiencing love/abundance and radiating it outward. I sometimes visualize the sun, infinitely full and radiating out.

Do the in breath/out breath shift at least three times in a row each time that you practice it.

During your in and out breaths, you can also meditate on phrases like these:

IN: I am open and willing to be fulfilled,
OUT: in all aspects of my life.

IN: I am worthy, safe, and loved,
OUT: an extension of God's love.

IN: I am my full Whole Self,
OUT: radiating love and abundance.

IN: I am an extension of infinite love and abundance,
OUT: experiencing it in all aspects of my life.

IN: I am filled with infinite abundance (or love);
OUT: I am sharing it.

IN: I am my Greater, Whole Self,
OUT: and I am living from Inner Wisdom.

IN: I am connected to Source,
OUT: experiencing abundance supporting me.

IN: I am my Whole Self,
OUT: experiencing myself in charge of my life.

IN: I am part of an abundant and supporting universe,
OUT: and I am sharing abundance and support.

IN: I am Spirit,
OUT: playing joyously with abundance.

You can use any wording that fits where you are and what you choose to have happen in your life. One useful measure is to take that which you choose to experience and make it your identity. For example:

IN: I am whole and fulfilled,
OUT: experiencing wholeness and fulfillment in the world.

Remember, when you are your Whole Self, you are already all; your job is not to get, but to remove the blocks to experiencing your wholeness and abundance.

The important thing here is to experience yourself shifting your mental state, your emotional state, and your identity. The shift process builds on the skills we have learned in the mastery process. This is different from saying affirmations, in that we are visualizing and *feeling* ourself as the Whole-Self identity while we are doing the in and out breaths. No matter what words you use, *experience* yourself being the Greater, Whole Self. You can use the NLP anchor from the previous exercise to assist in this.

The secret here is clear and strong intention, and practice. You are training yourself for the Olympics of being your abundant Whole Self. In this Olympics we are all winners, sharing love and abundance for all.

I use this exercise as often as I can. I do it while I am opening mail, or taking a walk, or driving my car, or fixing a meal. I do it first thing in the morning and before I go to sleep, times when the mind is more accessible than usual. At these times I close my eyes and do the exercise in a more meditative state, taking very deep breaths, holding them for as long as possible, and breathing out very slowly. Of course, when I am driving the car I keep my eyes open and do less deep breathing.

I have a quartz watch at home and in my office that I have set to sound a little beep on each hour. I use that as a reminder to do the switch exercise. When the watch goes off I stop what I am doing and do the shift breathing exercise at least three times.

## Exercise for Beginning Each Day

A good way to begin each day (after first doing the shift breathing exercise) is to state:

1. The kind of day you are choosing to have; and
2. That you will make all decisions today from your Whole Self.

Decide what kind of day you choose to have—a happy day, a peaceful day, an abundant day. Then resolve to yourself:

I will be vigilant witnessing myself and catch myself when or if I get off track. I will be particularly aware of the feeling quality of my day. When I am upset or angry, I know that I have gotten off track and it is time to stop and start anew. I will remind myself that *I can choose to see this differently.*

Any time we are feeling stuck, upset, or angry, it is time to remind ourselves that we have chosen to have a happy day, or whatever kind of day we chose, and then to do the shift technique to get back to our Whole Self—which by its nature is love, peace, harmony, joy, and abundance.

The following is based on an affirmation by Florence Scovel Shinn. I have taken the liberty of substituting the words "The Whole-Self" for "Thy." I like to say it in the morning.

*Thank you for this perfect day.*
*This is a day of completion.*
*The Whole-Self will be done.*
*Miracle shall follow miracle*
*And wonders shall never cease.*

# How to Stay in the Whole, Abundant Self

*Gratitude is not only the greatest of virtues, but the parent of all others.*—Cicero

*It is always with excitement that I wake up in the morning wondering what my intuition will toss up to me, like gifts from the sea. I work with it and rely on it. It's my partner.*—Jonas Salk

Graduation from the school of money freedom means living as the unlimited Whole Self, at least for longer and longer periods of our life. The unlimited Whole Self is always present; if we are unaware of it, it is only because we are blocking it out. We access the Whole Self by surrendering our limited perspectives and beliefs and ALLOWING the Whole Self to take charge of our life. Then inner power, joy, abundance, success, security, happiness, balance, and peace follow naturally as by-products. As we ALLOW ourselves to be the Whole Self, we ALLOW ourselves to have what we truly desire in life.

The human experience is by its very nature limited and divided into polarities of big/small, good/bad, light/dark, etc. The universal challenge, journey, and quest of human existence is to exist in this limited world and yet at the same time to transcend it by living and seeing from the perspective of the Whole Self. That is what Jesus meant when He suggested that it is possible to be *in this world but not of it.* We do this by ALLOWING the all-knowing and joyful Whole Self to direct our lives.

We stay in identification with the Whole Self by adopting the observer consciousness, which helps to keep us from becoming submerged in the drama of daily life. Meditation and prayer are also useful. Still other practices that maintain the stance of the Whole Self include noticing when we are coming from fear and choosing love instead; being honest and dealing with our fears rather than denying them and projecting them onto others; focusing the strength of our intention; and making and following our declaration to be our Whole Self.

Remember: this is not a linear goal-setting exercise in which we strive to get from "here" to "there." There is no "there" to get to: the Whole Self is already present. It is simply a matter of choosing to *be* the Whole Self again and again. Whenever you notice you have reverted back to the little self, lovingly choose again.

Practice seeing yourself as the Greater, Whole Self with a body, instead of identifying yourself as a body with a spirit. Wayne Dyer says that "we are spiritual beings having a human experience."We can think of ourselves as extensions of an energy that is connected with the energy of all other beings. We are cells in the body of the Universe.

The following are some principles that facilitate our being in our identity as the Greater, Whole Self:

*USE EMPOWERING LANGUAGE*

The language we use in both our inner dialogue and our spoken word creates our experience of life. Eliminate process expressions such as *I'll try* or *I am working on it.* Eliminate self-manipulation phrases like *I've got to, I have to, I must, I should,* and *I ought to.* As discussed in chapter 4, eliminate statements of feeling powerless before outside circumstances, people, and things; such expressions include *I can't, It's not my fault that ... They won't let me, I can't help it, I haven't a choice,* and *It is impossible.* Replace these phrases with empowering language, such as:

> *I can . . .*
> *I choose . . .*
> *I am . . .*
> *I take a stand to . . .*
> *I commit to . . .*

## FEEL GRATEFUL

When you feel lack and anxiety, the little self is firmly in control. When you focus on feeling full—grate-full and thank-full—you ALLOW the Whole Self to take over. Count your blessings. Giving thanks for all that you have opens the door and ALLOWS more to flow in. It is helpful to take a little time each morning and each night just to give thanks for the wonderful things in your life.

Focus on those things that you have and give thanks for them, and they will increase. It is helpful to write "Thank you" on checks, so that you feel the flow of giving and receiving.

## LISTEN TO INTUITION

Quieting the chatter and anxiety of the little self ALLOWS us to hear our intuition, or inner wisdom, which is the guidance of our Whole Self. From the perspective of the Whole Self, unimaginable breakthroughs are possible. As we have seen, Einstein and Mozart referred to this place of intuitive knowing as the source of their inspiration; financially successful people like John Scully and Oprah Winfrey have done so as well. The small, inner voice of intuition is the voice of the Whole Self, which is connected to Infinite Mind.

Learning to differentiate intuition from the little self's conditioned chatter is an art that takes practice. We can begin to develop this ability by asking our intuition for answers to questions about little things that aren't important. As we acquire the habit of asking and listening, we can begin to trust our inner voice on more important matters. The most accurate litmus test by which to identify the guidance of the Whole Self consists of the questions, *Will this bring me peace?* and *Is this answer coming from love or fear?* If the guidance is coming from love and peace, then it is the Whole Self talking.

### FROM THE HEART

In this society most of us are conditioned to give on the basis of the transaction model: we give in order to get something else in return. Our giving is often based on fear or a sense of lack. This is the little self operating. When we give from our hearts, with no attachment to getting anything in return, we ALLOW the Whole Self to take charge. In actuality, we always receive what we give, since we are all interconnected. Both Jesus and Buddha said, in their own ways, *You reap what you sow.* Sharing love and abundance ALLOWS us to receive love and abundance. As the saying goes, *What goes around comes around.* The more love we give, the more we receive. And the same is true for everything else that we give.

This is the metaphysical truth behind the practice of tithing. When we share ten percent of what we receive, we are identifying with the larger whole; doing so opens the channel whereby we also receive from the whole. If one loves and supports the whole, then one can also receive love and support from the whole. We do this by deliberately putting aside "me-against-the-world" thoughts and cultivating instead an attitude of love and support for others. When I made my $500,000 in two weeks, it was partly the result of my desire to support a loving cause. However, if we are tithing to get, we defeat our real purpose. The purpose behind the act is more important than the act itself.

### FOCUS ON BEING THE WHOLE, UNLIMITED SELF

Whatever you focus your attention on expands. When you focus on what is wrong or missing, you feed energy to those problems, and they tend to increase. You may block solutions merely because you are preoccupied with feelings of frustration and distress.

When you give time and attention to ALLOWING your Whole Self to manifest, it manifests. When you focus on feelings of joy and fullness, those feelings expand. When you feel confident and keep your attention centered on solutions, you ALLOW your Whole Self to show you possibilities that were not visible to your little self. And when you focus on your purpose and vision, you ALLOW your Whole Self to handle details in an inspired manner.

*LOVE AND ACCEPT YOURSELF SO THAT YOU CAN BE FULL AND GIVING*

Criticizing and judging ourselves and others blocks the Whole Self. Loving and unconditionally accepting ourselves ALLOWS the Whole Self to fill up our pitchers so that we can give to others. The Whole Self is like a nurturing parent with an unlimited supply of love and abundance. It is up to us to choose to ALLOW that love and abundance to flow in.

*SEE YOURSELF AS PART OF THE WHOLE, LIVING SYSTEM*

The little self sees itself as separate. This is the source of its feelings of fear, scarcity, and lack. When we acknowledge our interconnectedness and interrelatedness to all creation, we ALLOW the abundant, unlimited Whole Self to be present. We can see ourselves as part of the whole, like a cell in the body of the planet. We feel the whole planet experiencing love and abundance. Reframing our reality to ALLOW joy and abundance helps everyone else do the same, since we are all interconnected.

*LET GO AND TRUST*

Holding on to our anxiety and fears blocks our access to the Whole Self. Letting go and trusting ALLOWS the Whole Self to operate. Trust attracts an abundance of whatever we choose to have in life. Think of the Whole Self as an abundant river flowing through you. When your little self gets upset, it throws boulders in the way of the flow. When you relax and trust, you ALLOW the river of love and abundance to begin to flow back into and through you.

## ENJOY THE PROCESS RATHER THAN STRIVING FOR OUT-SIDE REWARD

Anxiously striving for a reward keeps us in the little self, which is the place of emptiness and getting. When we relax into enjoying the process of life—when we are enjoying the journey instead of worrying about our destination—we AL-LOW the Whole Self to take control, and the rewards that are the by-products of identifying with the Whole Self flow in naturally. Being unattached to the result doesn't mean that the result doesn't appear. We hold our vision and AL-LOW the feeling state and expanded perception of the Whole Self to let the result unfold naturally. I would never have allowed myself to bring in $500,000 in the stock market if my little self had been in charge. A result of that magnitude wasn't in my limited self's context of possibilities.

## SEE YOURSELF AND OTHERS AS THE WHOLE SELF

When we choose to see the Whole Self in ourselves and others, we ALLOW it to begin showing up. In India many people greet one another with the word *Namaste,* which means:

*I honor the place in you where the entire universe resides;*
*I honor the place in you of love, of light, of peace.*
*If you are in that place in you and I am in that place in me,*
*there is only one of us.*

## DO WHAT YOU LOVE TO DO AND ALLOW ABUNDANCE TO SUPPORT YOU

Each of us has unique gifts to share with world. When we are pursuing our life's purpose, we ALLOW ourselves to express an expanded level of creativity, imagination, and genius—all aspects of our Whole Self. Achievement, success, and abundance flow in as natural by-products.

## FEEL JOY, INNER PEACE, AND ABUNDANCE

Our feeling state is more important than our actions. Always ask yourself, *Why am I doing this?* Choose to do what brings inner peace. Choosing the joy-peace state ALLOWS the Whole Self to be present. Our feeling state attracts a corresponding experience in our external life. Joy and inner peace are the natural feeling states of our Whole Self.

### *BE IN "BEGINNER'S MIND"*

When you think of yourself as an expert, there is no room for new perspectives or for more learning. The closed mind is the ground of the little self, which tries to protect its limited perspective. Innovation and creativity come from the Whole Self. When we keep our mind open, so that we are always "beginners," we ALLOW the innovation, creativity, and expanded vision of the Whole Self to flow in. As Peter Senge of MIT has said, "Creative intellects are at peace with what they don't know. They are willing to not understand. You can't be intuitive if you're trying to be right."

### *BE IN THE ETERNAL NOW*

The past and future are only ideas in our mind. Fear exists when we are in the past or in the future. Fear is gone when we are fully in the present. We block our lives when we constantly fill our minds with thoughts of the past or worries about the future. Focusing on the eternal now ALLOWS us to know and express the wisdom of the Whole Self. Lord Martin Exeter, a contemporary sage, said, *"The present moment is our window into the infinite universe."*

### *OPEN YOURSELF TO RECEIVE NATURAL ABUNDANCE*

Most of the time we block our reception of abundance, love, joy, happiness, and peace. However, observing ourselves can help us notice if we are blocking or sabotaging ourselves, and we can choose again to be our Whole Self, which is naturally joyful and abundant. Abundance is our natural state when we allow ourselves to receive.

*BE THE CHANGE YOU WANT TO SEE HAPPEN*
This is graduation. It is about *being*, not *trying to get*. Step into the reality of being the Whole Self, of being abundant, of being joyful, of being peaceful, of being whatever you choose. The being state ALLOWS us to experience the Whole Self. The being state ALLOWS us to have what we choose in our outer life. Peace and abundance begin with you and me.

We can retrain the body so that feelings of joy and abundance are its natural condition. Studies in psycho-immunology have shown that our brains can become addicted to certain kinds of internally produced chemicals. We can become addicted to fear chemicals or joy chemicals. When we become used to joy chemicals, we have created a state in which we can be our Whole Self.

Dr. Paul Pearsall, in his book *Super Joy*, says, "We are all addicted to what seems 'normal' for us. We are pulled through life like puppets passively responding to chemical configurations established for us from inside our own brains... Super joy people experience a range of consciousness, living life on several levels and in different ways, knowing many realities and many worlds."

The process we have been describing is one of ALLOWING, not one of SEEKING. It is being full and whole and allowing that fullness to be mirrored in our external life. The direction is from inner to outer. Inner wealth leads to outer wealth. Inner power leads to feeling empowered and empowering others. Inner peace leads to the outer experience of peace.

Put a guard on the gate of your mind and refuse entrance to negative thoughts. Banish them and replace them with gratitude, abundance, appreciation, joy, celebration, and love. See yourself as an extension of the perfection of God's love, abundance, and harmony. Heaven is not a place to get to. It is an already-existing, ever-present state of mind and feeling. It is within.

Remember: Since the Whole Self is an extension of the perfection of the Creator, as we move into that expanded identity we don't *have* to do anything, and we *can* do anything and everything.

In meditation we ALLOW ourselves to dis-identify from the everyday world of physical form. One helpful meditation exercise consists of imagining oneself becoming the object that is being meditated upon. Any activity is helpful that assists us to transcend our feelings of separateness and helps us to access the Whole Self—whether it be a spiritual experience, letting ourselves go in listening to a piece of music, watching a sunset, loving our child as we care for her, or the sexual experience of sublime union.

One of the signs of being in the Whole Self is the appearance of synchronicities—those uncanny coincidences of outer and inner events that have no apparent causal connection but carry meaning or significant impact. Perhaps you've had the experience of wanting to get in touch with someone you haven't seen for months or even years; then that person unexpectedly calls on the phone or shows up in an airport where you are waiting for a plane. One day recently I realized that I needed the help of a computer expert; later the same day I was introduced to one at a meeting.

By moving into the identity of the Whole Self we increase the number of synchronicities in our lives. This can be very helpful. Sometimes when I'm hunting for a parking space I play a sort of game in which I release my anxiety, open up to the Whole Self, and ALLOW a vacant spot to appear. It is also possible, when you are delayed for an appointment, to ALLOW time to expand so that you are able to arrive on schedule. You can't do this if you are feeling anxious, because then the limited little self kicks in.

My friends and I often share stories of our impossible synchronistic events because those experiences are such fun and they remind us of the Whole Self and its level of reality. Synchronicities are part of the process whereby we attract opportunities that allow us to have abundance or whatever it is we are choosing.

The money-freedom approach to being is to relax and allow abundance to flow into our lives. As we swim with the current of life, let go, use our intuition, and trust, we are buoyed up in a greater flow that we could never understand nor manipulate with our meager intellects. As we see ourselves as part of the whole, it is easy to give and receive freely. We find joy, peace, and freedom through non-attachment to specific outcomes.

This is also the way of being that Jesus implied when He admonished us not to be anxious for the morrow, and that the *Bhagavad-Gita* refers to as taking action without concern with results. Indeed, the great teachers of humanity have exemplified this way of life throughout history. When we are not anxious about lack, we allow the natural abundance of life to flow through us. We are being in the midst of life's process, committing our energies fully, following our highest vision, and trusting—while letting go of any attachment to how the results look. This approach means moving from fixed, linear goals to a flexible, spontaneous stance that constantly allows fresh wisdom to come in from the unlimited Whole Self. When we are in the abundance flow, we identify with the whole, though we may for the moment see only our part in it.

# 12

## ENVISIONING AN ABUNDANT
## WORLD THAT WORKS FOR ALL LIFE

*I did not arrive at my understanding of the fundamental
laws of the Universe through my rational mind.*
—Albert Einstein

*Thought that is no longer limited, brings experience that is
no longer limited.*
—Marianne Williamson, *A Return to Love*

*The true nature of our ground state and that of the Universe is that it is a field of all possibilities . . .
From this level it is possible to create anything. This field is
our essential nature. It is our inner self.
It is also called the absolute, and it is the ultimate authority. It is intrinsically affluent because it gives rise to the
infinite diversity and abundance of the Universe.*
—Deepak Chopra, M.D., *Creating Affluence: Wealth
Consciousness in the Field of All Possibilities*

*LITTLE, LIMITED SELF:* It is a tough world where I can't
get enough of what I need.

*GREATER, WHOLE SELF:* I am whole and abundant,
a part of the Infinite love/ abundance energy of the Universe, in which an abundant world for all is possible.

*LESSON:* You are helping others as well as yourself by
expanding beyond the limited mind to the infinite field of
possibilities and envisioning an abundant world that works
for all.

IMAGINE THAT you are a magician and that you can animate objects. You have before you two tables of water pitchers and a third table filled with cups, all of which you are
going to bring to life.

On the first table there are ten water pitchers, each one-quarter full. There is a pail of water in the center of the table. The pitchers have to compete and jockey to get the scarce water.

The second table holds ten water pitchers, all completely full. In the center is a faucet that dispenses as much water as any pitcher wants, at any time.

The third table holds a hundred empty cups, each waiting to be filled by one of the pitchers from either table.

As you begin to animate the water pitchers in your mind, put yourself in their place. What are they feeling?

Do the pitchers at the first table have to defend their turf? Are they tense about lack? Do some feel like victims of an impossible system? Do they decide not to compete? Do others feel anxiety and pressure to get enough water to do their job? Do they judge which cups are worthy of the limited supply? Do they feel separate and fearful? Are they worried about the future supply of water?

Perhaps the pitchers on the second table are having fun creating new ways to fill the cups faster by cooperating and using ingenuity. It has become a challenge for them to invent a better way to fill the cups. They are all lovingly supporting one another and having a wonderful time.

Obviously, the abundance-for-all reality is more fun. Remember that abundance isn't the amount of money or stuff that a person stockpiles. According to *Webster,* abundance is *overflowing fullness.* It is the *feeling quality* of having enough and of trusting that we will always have enough. With this trust, we don't need to hoard or defend. We just act as a channel of the unlimited supply, a part of the great circle of giving and receiving.

"But," you say, "it can't be that way." Why not? Granted, it will take time to change our beliefs and the way we have structured our world. Yes, as long as we are looking out at the world from a small, limited mind, the realization of an abundant world for all is absolutely impossible. It cannot be created through minor adjustments to our society's structure. It cannot come through forcing people to use less and share more.

And yet, what is impossible in one paradigm may not be impossible in another. After all, if we had told the Pilgrims landing on Plymouth Rock that some day this country would put a man on the moon, they would have *known* that this was impossible. *The impossible becomes possible when we step outside the paradigm through which we are currently experiencing life.*

I invite you to join me in being a paradigm shifter. I invite you to participate in envisioning an abundant world that can work for all. This act of envisioning will not only help to bring the vision closer to possibility, it will also help you to release your own personal blocks to abundance.

Physics tells us the Universe is made up of energy. This energy is a field of infinite possibilities. We impose meaning and structure on the atoms and molecules of our world. Similarly, we create the structure of society through the action of our collective consciousness. Our either/or mind projects and thereby creates a split world. Our inner lack and limitation create a world of lack and limitation.

Therefore, to transform the world into one that is abundant and that works for all life, we begin by asking to *believe that it is possible;* then we proceed to transform ourselves into the Whole Self, using the Mastery Process.

Before anything else, we must allow ourselves to believe this transformation is possible. We create an open space, a beginner's mind, and allow ourselves to catch some glimpses of the higher intelligence. Each one of us can take this first step. As Vaclav Havel, the poet and former president of Czechoslovakia said, "Without a global revolution in the sphere of consciousness, nothing will change for the better in the sphere of our being."

## Leaving Our False Assumptions Behind

*And just as the false assumption that we are not con-*
*nected to the earth has led to the ecological crisis, so the*
*equally false assumption that we are not connected to*
*each other has led to our social crisis. Even worse, the*
*evil and mistaken assumption that we have no connec-*
*tion to those generations preceding us or those who will*
*follow us has led to the crisis of values we face today...*
*We can get along, yes, people of all backgrounds can not*
*only live together peacefully, but enrich one another,*
*celebrate diversity and come together as one. Yes, we will*
*be one people and live the dream that will make this*
*world free.*—Vice President Albert Gore, in his acceptance speech at the Democratic National Convention,
July 16, 1992

*We awaken from the dream that we are weak, and ac-*
*cept that the power of the universe is within us.*—A
Course in Miracles

Our society reflects our personal anxieties and limitations. We each spend our energy getting enough stuff or
defending our stuff, and on the national level an expanded
version of the same competitive game plays itself out. Defense expenditures in the world, even after the demise of
the Soviet Union, are still more than a trillion dollars per
annum.

We have created a "substance"—money—to facilitate the
exchange of goods and trade. This substance could have
functioned the way blood does in our own bodies, harmo-
niously nurturing all parts of the whole. Instead, we have
projected power, prestige, status, and happiness onto
money; we have become accustomed to seeing it as the
source of these things. We have made money a commodity
to be competed for, accumulated, and hoarded.

Why have we done this? Because of our underlying fears of scarcity and limitation. Given our present assumptions about the nature of reality, an abundant world that works for everyone is a mere pipe dream. So the first step is to change our erroneous assumptions about our identity and what *reality* is.

For three hundred years our society has operated on the basis of a set of assumptions that facilitated certain kinds of science, certain technologies, and certain economic processes, but which kept other possibilities limited. With the advent of twentieth-century science, these mechanistic assumptions have been shown to be true only within limited frameworks. Yet in many cases we still hold fast to them.

Here are some of the most glaring of our common *false assumptions:*

- That the world is divided into two separate and independent realms, mind and matter. Matter, we assume, is essentially dead, and the world of matter consists of separate bits and pieces that interact like the gears and wheels of a machine. Meanwhile, the world of the mind is seen as a fundamentally unreal realm that has no direct impact on matter, which constitutes a fixed reality *out there* that we can describe objectively.
- That we are isolated egos inside separate bodies, and that we are separate from God—or Source—from each other, from nature, and from money. This assumption has led us to believe that we must conquer nature, hoard money, create jobs, manipulate other people, and bully other nations. We see a fragmented world, a collection of separate objects, events, nations, races, religions, and political groups. We also see ourselves as fragmented—split into body, emotions, intellect, intuition, and so on. We then tend to identify ourselves with one fragment of our Whole Self: our physical being and its senses. This limited self-view blocks our experience of abundance because we project our

lack of wholeness out into the world. Because we see from a split mind, we see the world as a split, either/or place, where we can be *either* spiritual *or* wealthy; where we can *either* be a good person *or* sell out to money; where we can *either* keep our friends *or* have riches.

• That everything that happens is based on a definite cause having a definite effect.

• That human nature is immutable, ar.d that economics must be based on a human nature of greed, insatiable consumption, selfishness, and competition.

• That we are lacking, and we must strive to get what we need from others or from the outside world.

• That our lives are controlled by external persons and things.

• That the world is a limited pie, and we have to compete to get our piece of it; and that when we do, we are depriving someone else of that piece.

• That the source of all wealth, power, happiness, and worth is in the external world.

• That the only way to make our economy work is to promote more consumption.

• That the only way to understand, design, and predict an economic future is to use hard data from the past.

• That societal economic decisions have to be based on short-term goals that produce short-term positive results.

• That the goal and measure of economic progress is the gross national product, which is narrowly defined in terms of private-sector activities and cash transactions.

It is only when we realize that we are operating according to these assumptions that we can change them. Then a non-linear, quantum leap to a new reality becomes possible.

*This is how a human being can change*
*There is a worm*
*addicted to eating grape leaves*

*suddenly he wakes up*
*Call it grace, whatever,*
*And he's no longer a worm*
*He's the entire vineyard*
*and the orchard too*
*The fruit, the trunks,*
*a growing wisdom and joy*
*that doesn't need to devour*
                     —Rumi

## Healing Scarcity Consciousness for the Whole

*A human being is a part of the whole, called by us "Universe"; a part limited in time and space. He experiences himself, his thoughts and feelings as something separated from the rest—a kind of optical delusion of consciousness. This delusion is a kind of prison for us, restricting us to our personal desires and to affection for a few persons nearest us. Our task must be to free ourselves from this prison by widening our circle of compassion to embrace all living creatures and the whole of nature in its beauty. Nobody is able to achieve this completely but the striving for such achievement is, in itself, a part of the liberation and a foundation for inner security.*—Albert Einstein

*Relativity and quantum theory agree in that they both imply the need to look on the world as an "undivided whole," in which all parts of the Universe, including the observer and his instruments, merge and unite in one totality... the new form of insight can perhaps be called "Undivided Wholeness in flowing Movement"... In this flow, mind and matter are not separate substances. Rather they are different aspects of one whole and unbroken movement.*—David Bohm, *Wholeness and the Implicate Order*

According to modern physics, the Universe is a dynamic, indivisible whole, a vibrating web of energy patterns. It is a field of infinite possibility. We are not the separate, solid, material entities that we appear to be. Everything is interrelated with everything else. Since we cannot observe reality without changing it, we are part of the external world, not separate from it. As the Eastern mystics have said for centuries, all things are a manifestation of an underlying oneness. All seeming pairs of opposites are truly aspects of one underlying unity, like the two sides of a coin. And this multidimensional world of infinite energy is affected by our consciousness.

So: if the world isn't what we thought it was;
if it isn't what we were taught it was; and
if it isn't what it looks like to our physical senses;

WHO is to say what is possible or not possible when we shift from our limited-self outlook to being our Whole, Abundant Selves in a field of unlimited possibility? Twentieth-century science shows us that gradual linear change is not always the rule. Quantum leaps into new realities are possible.

We are subject to the laws of the Universe. But we need not be subject to the limited laws that we have made up as our apparent reality—what I call the laws of the illusion. *An abundant world that works for all is possible under the laws of the Universe.*

For me, the occurrences of synchronicity remind me of my true identity as the Whole Self in a Universe of infinite possibilities.

What is the purpose of having scarcity on the planet? Scarcity serves our limited self, which is striving to be okay by getting more than others have. It serves the fearful part of us, by proving that the world is a fearsome place. It serves the part of us that seeks safety in playing small, by providing us with an excuse for our inability to do things. It serves the part of us that believes we are separate, by proving that we are separate. It serves the part of us that believes in an either/or world, by proving that this view is accurate. A world of scarcity proves that our little, limited self is right. Would you rather be your little, limited self and be *right,* or would you rather be the Whole Self and be happy and abundant?

When we shift to knowing the Whole Self, these strategies make no sense. The way out of our problems is to be our Whole, Abundant Self, which is a whole within a world of wholes and sees no lack or need for lack. As defined by *Webster's Dictionary, whole* means "comprising the full quantity or amount, complete, undivided, a thing complete in itself, uninjured, unharmed, not fractional." When we experience ourselves as whole, then we can experience others as whole and the world as whole. As we heal ourselves, we extend healing to others. The origin of the word *whole* is *heill,* meaning "heal."

Chances are you have a hologram on your credit card. A hologram is three-dimensional image of an object produced using a laser beam. The interesting thing about a hologram is that if you cut it into pieces, each piece contains the entire image, though at a lower degree of resolution. It is still a whole, not a fragment. Some twentieth-century scientists have proposed that our brain stores information somewhat the way a hologram does—as a set of frequencies and wave patterns—and that the Universe itself may be a kind of hologram in which each part is a coarse-grained picture of the whole. According to this view, we are wholes within a whole Universe, not mere fragments that are by their nature utterly separate and different from each other and from their context.

*The shift from our present world of scarcity and crisis to an abundant, loving world that works for everyone is a function of our identity shift from the little, scarcity-conscious, separate self to the Whole, Abundant Self that is a part of the whole of all life.*

The Whole Self can throw away the old limiting script and create from the place of connection to the infinite wisdom of the Universe. As more and more of us shift from scarcity and fear to love, abundance, and trust, the doors will open to a new vision on the society level. Perhaps we should eliminate the very word *impossible* from our vocabulary, since it so often reinforces our limited, fragmentary identity.

Change proceeds from the inside outward. Needless to say, the outside change will reinforce the inner shift; but without a consciousness shift, outer reform is never really effective. While the change is working its way out, it is important to keep our attention on the process of inner transformation, rather than getting lost in matters of outer form. Designing the details of the structure merely brings us back into the little self. From that place, the best that we can do is merely to design a plan for yet another Utopia that can't work.

During a workshop, I asked the participants deliberately to take on the feeling of scarcity. Then we visualized a nature scene together. The participants had distressing experiences of polluted air and water and of vanishing resources. I realized afterward that our whole society is doing what we did in that workshop—applying scarcity consciousness to nature.

I belong to a transformational politics salon run by Gordon Davidson and Corrine McLaughlin. This salon brings together social activists and people from a variety of different spiritual paths. The purpose of the salon is to help us shift our perceptions of issues away from polarities so that we can see from a higher perspective, one that opens new possibilities. I did a visualization with the group, envisioning an abundant world that works for all life. Many people in the group were experts in technologies for a new and better world. Nearly everyone visualized scenes that epitomized simple human values. One person saw herself sitting in a town square talking to people of all ages; another was walking with his father in his rose garden; still another participated in a community art festival. Others saw people dancing in a large circle and children laughing and playing. All the activities involved people working or playing together, creating beauty or enjoying it. None of them focused on consuming, depleting the environment, accumulating money, or competing with others.

*Let's imagine that enough of us have shifted our identity to being the Whole, Abundant Self that society has begun to reflect this transformation.* In the new world we are creating together, this is what we might see:

• People are operating in an open system in which non-linear quantum leaps are the accepted norm rather than unusual occurrences to be met with resistance. They are creating their society from their connection to infinite intelligence, where their possibilities are unlimited.

• People are overflowing with peace, love, joy, and material well-being.

• Excessive consumption has fallen away because people no longer feel the need to fill an internal void. No one feels compelled to hoard or stockpile.

• The enjoyment and expansion of inner riches—spiritual fulfillment, loving relationships, and creative activities—have replaced consumption activities.

• People experience the world as a safe, loving, and nurturing mutual-support system. Because people feel safe, they no longer feel the need to devote resources to personal and national defense.

• Human beings don't pollute and consume Mother Earth, because they see themselves as cells in the one body of the planet.

• Some people have chosen to have more wealth than others, but there is enough for all to meet their needs.

• People are motivated by accomplishment and fulfillment rather than money, so they do what they love to do.

- Unimaginable discoveries are made that allow people to deal with physical problems—like their need for energy—without damage to the environment.
- Economic decisions are based on long-range results, freeing us to be productive in a way not imagined before.
- Money has returned to its original purpose as a neutral tool to facilitate trade. It operates like blood in the human body, moving substances to where they are needed for the good of the whole.
- Increased cooperation and teamwork have empowered people, stimulating creativity and productivity.
- Society's economic goals are based on values, fulfillment, and inner riches.
- People are happy, joyous, and free.

It is a lot more fun than the present game. As James P. Carse wrote in *Finite and Infinite Games*, "Finite players play within boundaries: infinite players play *with* boundaries ... The rules of a finite game may not change; the rules of an infinite game must change."

Biologist Rupert Sheldrake proposes that there are hidden fields, which he calls morphogenetic fields, that act on matter like a blueprint. The more often a specific form appears or behavior occurs, the more the field is enforced. The stronger the field, the more likely it is for the same behavior or form to appear in the future. Forms in different times and places affect each other by *morphic resonance.*

We can change the world when enough of us make a quantum leap into the transformed state. In her classic book *The Aquarian Conspiracy,* Marilyn Ferguson described a new kind of revolution that *looks to the turnabout in consciousness of a critical number of individuals, enough to bring about a renewal of society.* Her premise is that a critical number of people with a new perspective could trigger a basic shift.

This is the premise behind The Hunger Project, which was founded to be a catalyst for a paradigm shift. This international charitable project was launched by EST founder Werner Erhard in 1977 with the purpose of *making an idea's time come.* The Hunger Project assumes that hunger persists because of the age-old paradigm's assumption that it is impossible to feed the world's population. Experts claim that the know-how to end hunger in two decades does exist. In its first two years, the project already had enlisted seven hundred fifty thousand people who pledged their support to end hunger by the year 2000.

This project spawned many solutions. For example, Sam Harris founded the organization Results to create the international political will to end hunger. Results has been instrumental in getting various legislation enacted, such as microenterprise lending to empower people by helping them to become self-employed, rather than encouraging them to rely on government programs that reinforce the poverty cycle, as our welfare system does.

## Visualization: Abundance for All

*If the doors of perception were cleansed, man would see things as they are, infinite.*—William Blake

What would it be like to live in a world where you felt totally safe and unconditionally loved and accepted? What would it be like to live in a world where everyone felt safe and secure and loved by all? What would it be like to live in a world where people didn't have personal defenses and society didn't pour a major portion of its money into national defense? What would it be like to live in a world where all people were free to follow their highest purpose? What would it be like for everyone to be free of worries related to money and material needs? What would it be like if each person had enough and trusted he or she would always

have enough? What would it be like if all people were free to
focus their attention on the good of the whole, and all felt
identified with the whole? What would it be like to live in a
world where you "knew" that there was enough for everyone and that there would always be enough for everyone?

### Visualization

*Find a quiet place and sit down. Close your eyes, get com-
fortable, and relax. Take a deep breath, hold it, and let it out
very slowly. Continue exhaling even after it seems all the
breath is gone. Do this five more times.*

*Imagine yourself sitting at the seashore. The sun is shin-
ing, and you feel its pleasant warmth. There is a slight breeze,
and the temperature is just right. You see the magic sparkles
of the sun on the water. You listen to the constant breaking of
waves and the sounds the water makes as it gently rolls
ashore.*

*Take a deep breath, inhaling the fresh ocean air. Feel the
abundance of the ocean stretching out as far as you can see.
Feel the abundance of the air. Feel the abundance of sunlight
and the trust you have that the sun is always there, even
when you can't see it. Even when it is temporarily obscured, it
is always there with its light and warmth, waiting to shine
forth again.*

*Take another deep breath and press the fingers of your
right hand into the palm, bringing back the feeling of the
expanded Whole Self. Feel yourself expanding into the Whole
Self. Feel the infinite love of your Creator for you. Feel your
deep connection with the infinite energy of the Universe. Feel
the vibrating energy that is you and that connects you to all
life. Experience yourself as energy dancing in the cosmic
dance of life. Feel all the myriads of joyous expressions of the
One dancing together in a vibrant, interconnected whole.
Feel yourself full and overflowing with energy, and see everyone else the same way. Feel the joy of the complete freedom of*

*the dance. Feel the joy of being a part of an infinite interplay of harmony, love, and abundance.*

*See how this energy comes down into the level of form. See the people all holding hands in a joyous circle of diversity. Feel the connection you have with all. Feel the warmth of the sun, and see the blue sky. Hear the singing—even the birds have joined in! Notice the lush plants and trees covered with fruits. Feel the joy and trust there is here. Everyone has enough. It is the Garden of Eden!*

*Notice, as you look at each person, that your Whole Self is joyfully seeing that person's Whole Self. There is a feeling of unconditional love and acceptance and support. You feel that you are in a Universe that is a safe mutual-support system. You feel nurtured and loved. You know on a deep level that you have enough and that you will always have enough. You know that there is enough for all those smiling faces out there. You all have chosen to structure your world to love and support each other. If someone were to ask you what heaven is like, this is the way you would describe it.*

*There are people laughing and creating a multitude of beautiful arts and crafts. They have joy and pride in their work. Businessmen and scientists are cooperating and inventing breakthrough after breakthrough. It seems as though every day there are new announcements of marvelous breakthroughs in technology to make our world work better and to conserve the beauty of our natural wonders. You marvel at the infinite number of inventions—and at the fun people are having implementing them. Life is a harmonious, joyful experience. You feel gratitude to be alive now, in this new world of abundance shared by all.*

*Take a few minutes to stay in the feeling state of joy and abundance for all. Allow thoughts and pictures to come into your mind. Just notice them as they arise, without any judgment. Stay in this place as long as you choose.*

*When you are ready to come back, gradually begin to move your fingers and toes. When you open your eyes, you will feel*

*energized and wide awake. Become aware of your surround-*
*ings. Feel your body sitting. Remember where you are and*
*what clothes you have on. Now wake up, feeling wide awake*
*and refreshed.*

What thoughts and pictures came up for you? Just notice
them, without evaluation. Some people don't see any pictures, while others recall scenes of loving relationships or
natural beauty.

You may want to share this meditation with friends or a
study group you belong to.

Once when the great mythologist Joseph Campbell was
talking about the possibilities for our time, he spoke of *not a*
*handful, but a thousand heroes, who will create a future*
*image of what humankind can be.* I invite you to join with
me and others by accepting the vision that it is possible to
have an abundant world that works for all life. We don't need
to know the details of how such a world will look. The broad
purpose is enough, and our not knowing the details gives
space for our Whole Selves to create from our inner wisdom.

I invite you to join with me and others to envision ourselves healing the scarcity consciousness of the world. As
we move toward believing that this is possible, we help it
come about. We help to heal our own split mind, which
projects an either/or world. Let us move into our Whole Self,
connected to the field of infinite intelligence and infinite
possibilities. As we heal scarcity consciousness as it relates
to financial abundance, we also heal it around other areas
of life. And as *A Course in Miracles* reminds us, *When we are*
*healed, we are not healed alone.*

Join me. Envision it. *Believe* it is possible. *Feel* it is possible. *Allow* yourself as an individual to experience abundance while seeing yourself as part of the unlimited whole
that is experiencing abundance. *Expand* your concept of
possibility. *Expect* that we will find new sources of power,

new inventions that will open horizons that we can't even imagine. We all know the song that goes, *"Let there be peace on Earth, and let it begin with me."* I propose we add, *Let there be abundance for all, and let it begin with me.*

# Relevant Books Reading List

*A Course in Miracles*

Butterworth, Eric, *Spiritual Economics: The Prosperity Process*

Capra, Fritjof, *The Tao of Physics*

Carpenter, Tom, *Dialogue on Awakening: Communion with a Loving Brother*

Chopra, Deepak, M.D., *Unconditional Life*

Chopra, Deepak, M.D., *Creating Affluence: Wealth Consciousness in the Field of All Possibilities*

Dyer, Wayne F., Dr., *You'll See It When You Believe It*

Jampolsky, Gerald G., M.D., *Love Is Letting Go of Fear*

Jampolsky, Lee, Ph.D., *Healing the Addictive Mind*

Morgan, Marlo, *Mutant Message*

O'Lill, Ruth, *A Consumer's Guide to Hope*

Patent, Arnold M., *Money and Beyond*

Ponder, Catherine, *Open Your Mind to Prosperity*

Redfield, James, *The Celestine Prophecy*

Robbins, Anthony, *Unlimited Power*

Sinetar, Marsha, *Do What You Love to Do and the Money Will Follow*

Vaughan, Francis, and Roger Walsh, *Accept This Gift: Selections from A Course in Miracles*

Williamson, Marianne, *Return to Love*

Tom Carpenter's book may be ordered from: The Carpenter's Press, P.O. Box 3437, Princeville, Hawaii 96722.

Arnold Patent's book may be ordered from: Celebration Publishing, Route 3, Box 365AA, Sylva, NC 28779. 1-800-476-4785.

Ruth O'Lill's book can be ordered from A.R.E. Press, P.O. Box 656, Virginia Beach, VA 23451-0656. 1-800-723-1112.

# About the Author

Patricia Remele is a real estate entrepreneur, motivational speaker and president of Life Mastery, a company which specializes in helping people to actualize their potential. In addition to private consulting, she addresses a wide variety of audiences on money freedom and self-empowerment. She is a member of the National Speakers Association.

A former writer for the U.S. Senate Finance Committee, Patricia holds a B.A. from Cornell University, where she studied economics and psychology. She has studied various psychological and spiritual paths including est, a six-month training program at the Center for Attitudinal Healing, and *A Course in Miracles*.

## For Additional Information

Concerning speaking engagements, workshops, and tapes, please contact:

P.O. Box 1101
Greenbelt, MD 20768
Fax: (703) 893-9750

# What Is A.R.E.?

The Association for Research and Enlightenment, Inc. (A.R.E.®), is the international headquarters for the work of Edgar Cayce (1877-1945), who is considered the best-documented psychic of the twentieth century. Founded in 1931, the A.R.E. consists of a community of people from all walks of life and spiritual traditions, who have found meaningful and life-transformative insights from the readings of Edgar Cayce.

Although A.R.E. headquarters is located in Virginia Beach, Virginia—where visitors are always welcome—the A.R.E. community is a global network of individuals who offer conferences, educational activities, and fellowship around the world. People of every age are invited to participate in programs that focus on such topics as holistic health, dreams, reincarnation, ESP, the power of the mind, meditation, and personal spirituality.

In addition to study groups and various activities, the A.R.E. offers membership benefits and services, a bimonthly magazine, a newsletter, extracts from the Cayce readings, conferences, international tours, a massage school curriculum, an impressive volunteer network, a retreat-type camp for children and adults, and A.R.E. contacts around the world. A.R.E. also maintains an affiliation with Atlantic University, which offers a master's degree program in Transpersonal Studies.

For additional information about A.R.E. activities hosted near you, please contact:

A.R.E.
67th St. and Atlantic Ave.
P.O. Box 595
Virginia Beach, VA 23451-0595
(804) 428-3588

A.R.E. Press

A.R.E. Press is a publisher and distributor of books, audio-tapes, and videos that offer guidance for a more fulfilling life. Our products are based on, or are compatible with, the concepts in the psychic readings of Edgar Cayce.

We especially seek to create products which carry forward the inspirational story of individuals who have made practical application of the Cayce legacy.

For a free catalog, please write to A.R.E. Press at the address below or call toll free 1-800-723-1112. For any other information, please call 804-428-3588.

A.R.E. Press
Sixty-Eighth & Atlantic Avenue
P.O. Box 656
Virginia Beach, VA 23451-0656